Conclusion

INTRODUCTION

Welcome to the beginner's guide for Cricut Design Space. As you may know, Cricut is a system used for design and cut projects. It gives you the possibility to make numerous DIY projects ranging from cards, invitations to vinyl designs and much more. No matter what creative idea you might have, you can probably make it with the help of Cricut. To be able to put your ideas out into the world, Cricut offers a free online software called Cricut Design Space.

Cricut Design Space is a PC programming system made by Provocraft, the designers of the Cricut machine. While the machine itself enables the client to cut different shapes and textual styles in a fury of sizes, the Cricut Design Space takes it to an unheard level. Just interface the Cricut to the PC through a USB port, introduce the product, and release a totally different element of making.

The principle advantage of the Cricut Design Space is the capacity for clients to weld, or associate letters together to frame a solitary cutting. Gone are the times of sticking each letter each one in turn. Presently letters, expressions, and shapes can be welded together before cutting, making it quicker and simpler than any time in recent memory to add cuttings to ventures.

Another advantage of the Cricut Design Space is that the shapes and letters can be controlled widely before cutting. Clients are never again restricted to just modifying the size, yet would now be able to change the shape properties to all the more likely help their general design. Each picture can be extended, inclined, and turned to get the accurate look the crafter is requiring.

While the Cricut Design Space has many benefits, my undisputed top choice is the capacity to fuse pictures from different cartridges into one design. The client would now be able to design with all the cartridge choices without a moment's delay as opposed to being constrained to cutting with one cartridge at any given moment.

Speaking of machines that make for all the amazement, functionality, and effectiveness, the Cricut cutting machine is undoubtedly one of them. This, in part, is because of the underlying Cricut Design space, a free of charge mobile application that literally makes things magical happen.

This tool, in all ramifications, is significantly easy to use. But mastering how to actually use this user-friendly app is not something that can happen in 24 hours. If at all you want to go from a new user to a fairly advanced Cricut Design Space user in a matter of weeks or months - depending on your pace - you will have to know just how to go about it.

Cricut Design Space lets you choose from a pool of more than 50,000 high-quality images and other projects in the Cricut Image Library. If you want to use your own images and fonts, you can also do so at no cost. You can upload and clean up your own images, have a go at designing and cutting without needing an internet connection.

Cricut Design Space also gives you what you need to put your creative juices to the test in the niches of fashion, jewelry, and scrapbooking. If you never used Cricut Design Space before but wish to know how to start your own projects and create amazing designs in no time, you've come to the right place. This guide will show you everything you need to know, and it will finally give you the possibility to use your creativity to its fullest.

This guide was intended for beginners. Even if some information will seem obvious at times, please consider that the experience of users might differ. This guide should be accessible and easy to understand to everyone willing to learn. That way, any guesswork will be completely taken out and you can emerge from this experience with a solid foundation in Cricut Design Space. Now, without further ado, let's dive in and start our journey.

Chapter 1: What Is a Cricut Machine?

Cricut has for some time been a popular brand under crafted by Provo Craft. Many individuals have long overlooked the craft of scrapbooking and paper patterns, as people dive into the new universe of advanced workmanship and makeovers. Luckily, there are still organizations like Cricut, who has high respect with regards to the customary types of expressions and artworks. For over forty years, Provo Craft had the option to give probably the most dazzling centerpieces roused by the most splendid wellsprings of imagination. Being a universal producer, the creators of Cricut have gradually extended to various pieces of the globe, giving boundless chances to numerous craftsmen and vendors. With its responsibility to give simply the best in the field of expressions and artworks, Cricut had the option to dispatch the absolute most surprising materials that are viewed as the must-have accumulation for each craftsman.

One of the most prevalent of the Cricut items is the Cricut shaper machine. By introducing a cartridge into the shaper, different shapes and plans can be made by any devoted specialties laborer. A ton of people set aside a ton of cash for this gadget, given its extraordinary guide with regards to planning. There are additionally the individuals who like to utilize the Cricut Expression line that digs in progressively expound designs, including silk screens and the utilization of vinyl and card stock. All machines are additionally utilizing the cartridges made by Cricut to concoct different themes and layouts.

In the event that you are progressively agreeable in utilizing the machine through the PC, you can likewise buy a duplicate of the Cricut Design Studio programming that enables you to match up Cricut slicing machines to your PC. This product incorporates an immense gathering of all pictures that are a piece of the Cricut cartridge library. Rather than looking through each cartridge inside your cabinet, you can now rapidly make your inquiry through an advanced gadget that will make the plans for you. You will in any case have the option to make a similar impeccable shapes and textual styles that you have constantly cherished with Cricut. Given your on-screen cutting mat, you will currently have the option to appreciate the advantages of pretty much every cartridge without experiencing all the messiness in the conventional method for expressions and artworks.

There are several electronic die-cutting machines. The Cricut machine is one of best of the lot. It is used by paper crafters, card makers, and scrapbookers.

Imagine a printer where you create the specific design you want on the screen. Once you are done with the design or image you want, you then proceed by instructing the machine to cut out the design. This is the simplest way to explain a Cricut machine.

A Cricut machine has the capacity to cut materials ranging from paper to faux leather, just to mention a few. In case you don't have good handwriting, you can also use this machine to that effect. In other words, you can make a Cricut do the job of a printer for you.

This is possible loading a marker in the accessory slot of the machine. When you do this, you can then proceed by making the machine draw the design you desire. Hence, the Cricut machine is also a multifaceted machine that is designed to bring some versatility to your table.

Designs written by loading the marker of the accessory slot of the Cricut machine are always exquisite. Interestingly, you don't have to even use physical cartridges with some versions of the Cricut machine! The Explore series is a typical example of such versions of Cricut machines.

These series of Cricut machines are designed such that you can use the online design software instead. What this implies is that any shape or text you desire can be selected from this platform. The specific design you want can then be sent to the machine in order for you to cut it out.

Interestingly, the Explore series of the Cricut machine also makes it possible for direct upload. Hence, you can simply upload the particular design you want and use the machine to cut it out. Cricut Machines are essentially a die-cutting machine. You can think of it like a cutting machine or a craft plotter. It is a printer that allows you to create a design or image on your computer, send it to the Cricut, and it prints and cuts the design for you. You can use any material to print and cut. The newer models of the Cricut, you can use vinyl, paper, fabric, sticker paper, craft foam, and even faux leather.

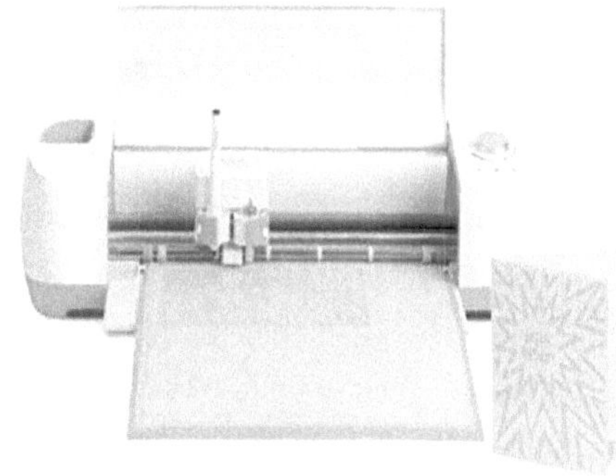

You can use a Cricut machine like a printer too. In the machines, there is an accessory slot which you can use to load a marker and have the machine 'draw' your design for you. If you love handwritten quotes and such, this is a perfect way of getting your handwriting font on your craft.

The Cricut can be used for plenty of different designs so long as your creativity permits. All you need is an idea, your creativity, a space for your craft, your material to cut as, well as your trusty Cricut machine.

What Crafts Can I Do with a Cricut Machine?

As mentioned previously, the possibilities are endless with the Cricut machine. As more and more crafters come on board with, they use their Cricut, more and more projects and crafts are created—look at Pinterest to see the myriad of ideas.

However, there are a few common and popular types of craft that all kinds of crafters take on when they begin using the Cricut to get the hang of it and understand its potential. If you have a Cricut machine, here is what it can do:

- Use it for scrapbooking—you can cut unique and intricate shapes and letters

- Create special occasion, custom cards that are 100 percent handmade

- Create a beautiful, personalized onesie or t-shirt

- Make a handmade leather bracelet

- Create amazing party decor from buntings to flags and party signage

- Create your stencils for painting

- Design and cut your very own vinyl stickers for your windows

- Use the Cricut to create cute labels for the playroom and pantry

- Design beautiful monogrammed pillows

- Craft your own Christmas ornaments that fit your theme

- Create beautifully addressed envelopes

- Decorate a mug, cup, or tumbler

- You can use it to etch your favorite glasses right at home

- Craft wall decals

- Create wooden painted signs for weddings, birthdays, or even for a hotel or inn

- Make your very own window clings

- Cut your own quilt squares or appliques

- Create beautiful decals for your laptop, stand mixer

There are plenty of crafts that you can create with your Cricut—it makes crafting easier, simpler and faster using this machine. If you are new to using the Cricut, fret not. In this book, you will be given the basics of the machine and how to use it appropriately. You will also be introduced to common, everyday crafts for beginners to give you a good understanding of the Cricut Machine. Doing common crafts will help you understand your machine and potentially lead you to explore what other things you can do with it.

How the Cricut Works?

When you see the finished product from a Cricut machine, you will definitely be blown away. The neatness and appealing look of a typical project done with the Cricut machine will take your breath away. However, only a few people understand the process involved in the creation of such amazing designs.

Curious to know how the Cricut machine is able to cut out materials effectively? You are reading the right book. There are three major steps involved when using the Cricut machine:

Have a Design

If you have a PC, you can access the Cricut Design Space to access the library of designs. If you have a Mac, you can access the same platform to select a huge variety of designs. In case you don't have any of these two but possesses an iPhone or iPad, you can use the Design Space for iOS.

If what you have is an android, you are covered as well. This is because you can take advantage of the Design Space for Android. These are online platforms where you can select any design that best suits your taste.

You can also customize a ready-made design to suit your need. For example, you can resize it or modify the shape. You can also add a text or image as you wish till you have the design just as you want it.

Prepare the Machine

Having selected the design you intend cutting out with the machine, you are ready for the next step. The machine needs to be prepared by turning it on. Once you switch on the machine, you actually don't need to do anything.

You don't have to press any button unless you are using the machine for the first time. In that case, the machine will give you instructions on what to do. It is that simple.

That is why both beginners and experts can make use of the Cricut machine without issues. Your computer or phone will have to be paired with the machine via Bluetooth for the first time. However, this will not be needed subsequently because the machine will remember the pairing.

Hence, once the machine is switched on, the pairing between the phone and the machine becomes automatic. The implication of this is that once the machine is switched on, the machine is ready. The next step is to send the design to the machine.

Send the Design to the Machine

The first thing the software does is to preview the various mats you have. A mat represents a sheet of material; hence, having two different colors in your project implies two mats. There are times that your project can be a combination of a fabric and a paper.

During such occurrences, you will have a mat representing each material utilized for the project. Once you have prepared the machine, you need to decide the dimension with which the machine will do the cutting. If you intend making two cards, the machine has to be instructed to make two project copies.

You will find this option at the top left of the Cricut Design Space. Most of the materials you will be cutting will be cut at 12" × 12" size. This is because this is the standard size that is the most prominent on the Cricut machine.

However, if you prefer a different dimension, you can always alter it. The mirror switch has to be flipped to mirror the design you want in case you want an iron-on design. This has to be done to guarantee that the alteration is reflected by the finished project.

Once you are set to send the design to the Cricut, you will click Continue. This option can be seen at the bottom right corner of the Cricut Design Space. It is easy to continue at this point because the software will prompt you to take you through what ought to be done.

Don't get what up about how to set up different projects of different materials and colors. This is because the instructions you need will be displayed on the screen, and you can easily follow through. Once you follow the instructions presented to you by the machine, you are guaranteed of top-quality cuttings.

The machine will request that you pick the particular material you want to use for the first mat. Simply choose whether it is paper, vinyl, fabric, leather, or any other material. Once you do this, the machine will automatically adjust pressure, speed, and the brush blade as necessary.

Hence, just ensure you do your part of instructing the machine to do your bidding as desired. You can trust the Cricut machine from that point to do all that is needed for a perfect project. After the machine has adjusted itself to cut, you will put the material into the Cricut cutting mat.

The machine will proceed to cut out the mat. The pieces that have been cut out can then be gathered by you and used as desired. This is how the Cricut machine works, and it is basically the same principle for every project.

Chapter 2: Buying the best Cricut Machine

The Cricut machine isn't actually the least expensive. One unit is about on the $300 value run, and what precisely isn't the friendliest cost. To get the best on estimating, you can generally do brisk hunts on the web, for example, eBay and other related destinations. You can likewise however at shopping center deals if web based purchasing alarms you somewhat. Keep in mind, it about looking and being tolerant simultaneously. Upbeat scrapbook making!

Your budget and how you intend to use the machine are big factors; however, you'll find most Cricut machines are around the same price with the exception of the Cuttlebug Machine.

This is a small, portable hand-crank machine that has a maximum cutting width of six inches. It only works with dies and embossing folders; however, it's perfect for those who are looking for a machine they can use for scrapbooking and card making.

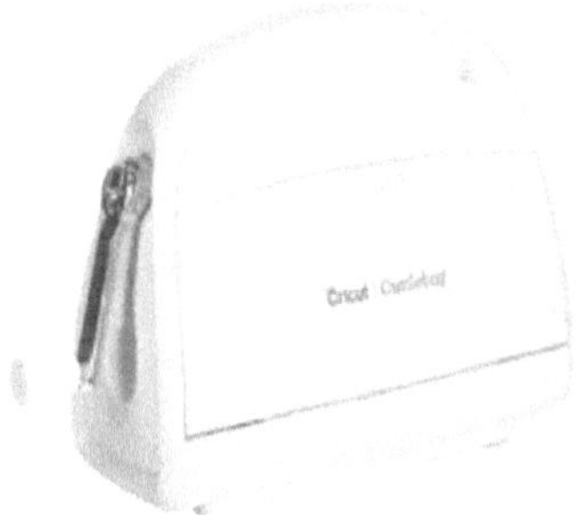

The hand-crank machine has been a staple in the Cricut family and you can usually find a new one for under $100. A used hand-crank can be far less money. If it's in good condition and that's what you want, you can sometimes find them for as low as $25 at garage sales and garage sale sites.

Cricut maker

This year, a new model was released called The Cricut Maker™. This has all the bells and whistles to do most anything. It has the capability of cutting more materials than any previous models and the company boasts its fast, precise cutting.

The Cricut Maker is considered to be Cricut's flagship model. This is the one that can do just about anything under the sun on just about any material you can fit into the mat guides of your machine. The one drawback of this powerhouse model is the price point. This does make this model more prohibitive, unless you plan to make crafts that you can sell with this model. If this is your intention, you can rest assured that whatever you turn out with this machine will be the best of the best, every single time. If you're selling your crafts, this baby will pay for itself in little to no time at all.

That in mind, the Cricut Maker costs $399.99. That is a large sum of money for someone who doesn't have it and even to someone who does have it. Although there's a lot you can do with $399.99, there are just as many things you can do with the Cricut Maker. My advice would be to save until you can afford it or put it on your wishlist in the meantime and subtly hint to your loved ones that you'll absolutely love to have one of these bad boys. Hopefully, someone will catch on and not balk at the huge amount of dollars that it will eat up.

The Cricut Maker can be used with your own images, which is a plus for those who prefer to use their own or don't want to buy a subscription or pay for individual images. It allows you to personalize your items and make your own statement. You can make personalized cards, signs, and anything your heart desires. The ability to personalize your items with multiple lines and fonts broadens your horizon, and if you make products to sell, you can offer personalization.

Cricut Cake

If you do manage to find either one of these machines, you can expect the price to amount to nothing less than $142.99 for the Cricut Cake Mini and $199.99 for the Cricut Cake Personal Electronic Cutter.

All in all, I think that if you can get your hands on the Cricut Cake, that will be incredible. It's not without its faults, but for a cake decorator and simple crafter, the Cricut Cake is perfect. The materials above can be cut just as good as with any other machine if you switch out the blade and use the right pressure, speed, and mat. You might struggle with slicing items that the machine was not designed to cut, though, so keep that in mind. There will be a limit when it comes to the variety of materials that you will be able to craft with, but it does work just fine with the things listed above.

The Cricut Cake is perfect for cutting unique details for any cake that you are decorating, especially for lettering and making silhouettes that are difficult to free-hand. The fondant cutouts can also be used to dress up cupcakes. Whatever the occasion may be, the Cricut Cake machine can cut your decorative fondant or gum paste perfectly.

With all the capabilities of the Cricut Explore One and more, the Cricut Explore Air model comes equipped with Bluetooth capability, has a built-in storage cup to keep your tools in one place while you're working, so they won't roll away or get lost in the shuffle.

This model does have two on-board accessory clamps, which allow for simultaneous marking and cutting or scoring. These clamps are marked with an A and a B so you can be sure your tools are going in the right places, every time you load them in.

This model is equipped to handle the same 100 materials as the Cricut Explore One, and operates at the same speed, so the price difference reflects those differences *and* the similarities! This is a great value for the powerhouse that you're getting.

At the time of writing this, the cost for the Cricut Explore Air is $249.99

Cricut Explore One

In terms of what is currently available from Cricut, this is the most basic machine they offer. This machine boasts being able to cut 100 of the most popular materials that are currently available to use with your Cricut machine, as well as being perfectly user friendly.

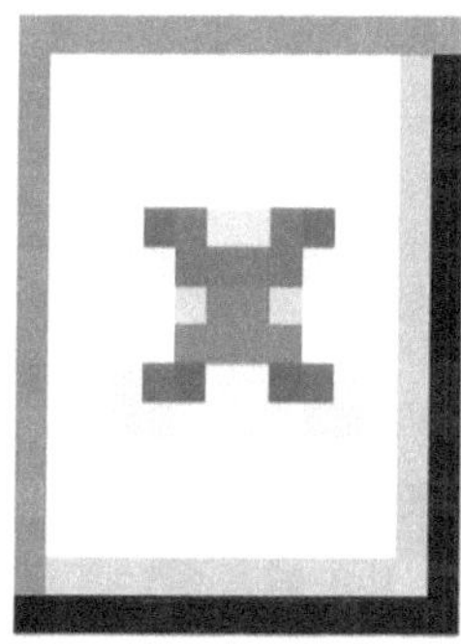

The Cricut Explore One is considered to be the no-frills beginner model of Cricut craft plotters and operates at a lower speed than the other models available. Unlike the others available in the current product line, the Cricut Explore One has only one accessory clamp inside, so cutting or scoring, and drawing cannot be done simultaneously. They can, however, be done in rapid succession, one right after the other.

While this is a great tool for a wide range of crafts on 100 different materials, and which can get you well on your way to designing breathtaking crafts that are always a cut above others, the cost is not as high as you might imagine. If you intend to use your craft plotter mainly for those special occasions where something handcrafted would be perfect, then this a great machine to have on hand. The cost for the Cricut Explore One is $179.99

This model cuts materials at twice the speed of the previous two models, has Bluetooth capability, and has the two on-board accessory clamps.

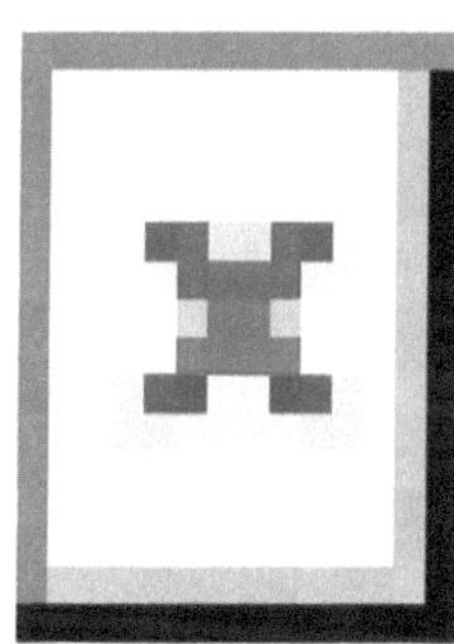

The storage cup on the top of the machine features a secondary, more shallow cut to store your replacement blade housings when they're not in use, so that if you happen to be swapping between several different tips for a project, they're all readily available to you throughout your project. Both of the cups have a soft silicone bottom, so you won't have to worry about the blades on your machine becoming dull or scratched!

For someone who finds themselves using their Cricut with any regularity, this is the best machine for the job. You will be able to do your crafts twice as fast, and you will get a satisfactory result every time, even at that speed!

At the time of writing, the Cricut Explore Air 2 is priced exactly the same as the Cricut Explore One, at $249.99. If you're looking to jump on this, now is the time to get the best deal.

Whatever you can afford. There is really no wrong way you can go. It all depends on what you want to do with the machine and how much money you are willing to spend.

Choose wisely

It takes structures that you make or transfer (like those you get free from us) into their Design Space programming and removes them.

Would you be able to transfer my pictures to use with Cricut?

Indeed! You can transfer your pictures, or any of our free SVG and Me cut records that are as of now arranged to be perfect with Cricut Design Space.

What various materials would i be able to cut with Cricut?

Everybody will in general consider Cricut machines as cutting paper or vinyl, yet the fact of the matter is there are a LOT more things that a Cricut can cut. The Cricut Explore Air 2 can cut more than 60 sorts of materials!

Will it be simple for me to figure out how to utilize Cricut Design Space to make my custom ventures?

That's right, and I'm here to help! Look at our Cricut instructional exercises page here, which is a great spot for learners to begin! We include new recordings every week and even give accommodating free assets and agendas, so ensure you return frequently.

With the current line of available models, the Cricut Design Space allows you to be an innovative as you can possibly be with the design process, so none of your creative flow is eaten up by operations that should be taken care of by your machine.

Chapter 3: Tools and Accessories to Use with a Cricut Machine

When you have a Cricut machine, there are a few tools that you would need which would make your crafting project easier and manageable. All these different tools help with cutting materials. The tools that you would need are:

Cricut Cutting Mat

For every Cricut Machine you have, the must-have item every crafter needs is a cutting mat. This cutting mat enables you to hold any material you use while the machine goes through cutting it. These mats come in different grip strength and also varying sizes. You can differentiate it by the colors it comes in based on the grip, so you do not confuse them. Some projects would require you to use the StrongGrip mat, whereas some projects work better using a mat suitable based on the materials you are using, such as fabric.

The outcome of your project depends on the kind of mat you use so choosing the right mat is imperative. The different types of mats available are the LightGrip Mat, StandardGrip Mat, StrongGrip Mat, and the FabricGrip Mat.

Cricut Bright Pad

This Bright Pad includes a five-brightness setting adjustable LED light. It makes your crafting easier, and it aids in illuminating extremely fine lines for tracing. It is extremely useful when you are weeding so if you do find that weeding is a challenge, then the Cricut Bright Pad will solve this issue for you as it makes this process easier.

Cricut Pens

Cricut Pens come in different colors and a variety of sets that make DIY projects such as gift tags, cards, invitations, and banners so much more creative and beautiful. Crafters usually use these pens when they need to Write and Cut. You can get the Metallic pens, Candy Shop pens, the Classic set, Gold set, and even one called the Seaside set.

Lint Roller

Yes, you read that right, get yourself a lint roller. It is useful for removing any unwanted pet hairs, dust or excess materials from your mats. Animal hairs are big problems as they stick to the adhesive mats like there is no tomorrow, but a lint roller works great if you want to get rid of them.

Scoring Stylus

Add a scoring stylus to your cart as soon as possible if you are a paper crafter. The tool is excellent for making paper baskets and boxes. It gives the products the professional, store-bought finish and makes them so easy to fold as the stylus already creates the grooves for folding your paper projects.

EasyPress

Invest in an EasyPress. This is perfect if you are interested in printing T-shirts or customizing pillowcases. Basically, anything you want to have printed, you are going to need one of these bad boys to do it. There are lots of bundles available on the Cricut website, and they can range from $119.99 (only the EasyPress) to $389.99 for a large bundle with everything you need to get started on your printing journey and so much more. The prices change depending on the size of the EasyPress, as well as the size of the bundle you wish to take.

Complete Starter Kit

The Complete Starter Kit is great if you don't feel like purchasing tools individually or if you'd rather follow protocol and purchase exactly what you need. The kit comes with all the essential items; that's why it is a great purchase. However, if you're tight on cash, buying the bare necessities will be best. This includes the materials you may require to start crafting so you don't have to worry about any list of items that need to be bought.

Cartridge

Cartridges are designed to help with the keyboard overlay that is needed for designs. The DesignStudio that is downloadable on the computer will help with developing the design that you are looking for. Each cartridge is designed to have a booklet to help you with how to use it. Each cartridge will only work for that specific overlay; however, a company called Provo Craft designed a universal overlay cartridge that will help with this single-use overlay issue. This allows the DIY crafter to only have to learn one keyboard overlay instead of multiple, giving them a much better chance of being able to learn the Cricut machine easily. Each Cricut, whether a cake version or a paper version, has a specific set of parameters that will be set to use for cutting. This makes each one of the Cricut machines specific to their use and a unique tool to have.

Buy a cartridge or several. Please do invest in these. They are amazing, and they aren't that expensive if you look around for clearance sales or marked-down prices on Amazon. There are so many cartridges to choose from; it's like a never-ending pit of creativity. The selection ranges from themed cartridges to ones that only have fonts. It's great for any project, and it saves you the trouble of struggling with Design Space and creating your own designs. They also come in neat little boxes that are so easy to store and always looks uniform.

Sharpies

Sharpies - you will not be sorry that you have them. Yes, the Cricut pens are cool, but they are overpriced. Purchasing some extra Sharpies – or any form of pens that can be manipulated into fitting into the pen holder – will work perfectly. You will have a variety of colors and save a couple of bucks in the process.

Doors

The door on your Cricut Cutter machine protects the machine when not in use. On many Cricut Cutter machines in various models, there is a compartment on the inside of the door to place any needed tools for crafting. If the doors on your Cricut cutter machine are not staying shut, make sure that you have taken out or unloaded any accessories in the machine's accessory clamp which can cause the doors to remain open. If this is not the case or the doors of the machine will not open or stay open take a picture or video and send it to the Help Center at cricut.com.

Spatula

For lifting cut peace of papers from the cutting mat spatula is used. Other related things like some stuffed card can be used. But, as spatula is not expensive and specially designed tool, so its use is recommended. It does not harm your cutting mat. Removing gross and sticky material from spatula is easy.

Adhesives

Glue, gums are adhesives, choose adhesive of your choice from any well-known brand. Sticky material like adhesives should not be ordinary, purpose of sticking two things together must be fulfilled through your selected adhesive. Different sizes of glue coffee cups are available. Select any jumbo pack or coffee cup or according to you requirement. The drying time of glue also matters, so go for some very good adhesive.

Tapes

Without tape completing task is almost impossible. Consideration Points for selecting tape are: it should be chemical or acid free and it should be very sticky. Glue is alternate for tape but sometime glue also does not work like tape.

Scissors

Keep a pair of sharp scissors with you. Enough sharp to cut cards, ribbons and papers. Must buy a cover for scissors. Place it above the reach of children and in a place where humidity does not affect it. Neat paper or card cutting really affect your decorative work.

Tweezers

Sometime you need to deal with very tiny papers. Tweezers work efficiently in holding that small piece of papers which usually turns, curves and torn during use. Sometime additional use of glue sticks two papers which are difficult to get separate tweezers are perfect helper at that time. Keep it while doing crafting you will must be needing it.

Trimmers

Blades and trimmers are essential thing it helps in cutting papers very neatly and in desired shape without putting additional effort to create neat effect.

Stock of paper and cards Card are comparatively thicker than paper. They are different things. Buying a stock makes you tension free, either you do test cuttings or throw it in making unusual shapes for trail. They should be sufficient for, until your whole tasks get complete.

Blades

The blades are designed to cut specific textiles when using the Cricut. Every single Cricut machine that you can buy comes with your own specific blade for that machine. You can purchase other blades that would be even more useful for specific textiles. Many of them come with a German fine point carbide blade. This is a useful blade for all projects. However, you may want to invest in a deep cut blade eventually. This one provides an effortless cutting of a much thicker textile such as leather and wood. There is an individual housing that will be used for this specific blade that is different from the one that comes with your machine, so keep that in mind. There is also an option or a fabric blade that is bonded. This is used to cut fabrics that are already stabilized with some sort of heat-pressed bonding. In the Cricut Maker, you will get a knife blade and a rotary as well. These do not work in other Cricut machines though.

Keypad

As mentioned in the previous paragraph the Cricut cartridge contains fonts and images often in a specific theme. The keypad allows you to input phrases and words to tell the Cricut what to cut out using the font in the cartridge.

For the most part, all buttons are self-explanatory the on button turns the machine on, the Cut button tells the machine to Cut once the design is already in place, and the Stop button tells the Cricut machine to stop cutting once the design has been fully cut. It is important to not try to Cut or press the Cut button without a cutting mat in place and without a design and cartridge ready to go. Select the STOP button if you've made a mistake during the cutting process, the blade will stop cutting and from there you can correct your mistake. The Off button turns the machine off.

Roller Bar

The roller bar piece of the Cricut Cutter machine has wheels called star wheels. Star wheels allow materials to not shift when cutting. However, when cutting thick materials like felt and foam the star wheels can leave marks and indents in the material. To avoid this marking from the star wheels moves the star wheels all the way to the right side of the rubber bar one by one. If the cartridge is in the way of this maneuver turn your Cricut Cutter Machine off by selecting the OFF button and gently move the cartridge over to either side. To make sure that the material still is not passed over by the star wheels make sure the material has at least one inch away from the right side of the rubber bar where the star wheels are now located.

Display Screen

The display screen on your Cricut Cutter machine shows the design in which the machine will be cutting. The design can be edited on the display screen. Settings for your Cricut machine are also accessible through the display screen, such as: calibrating the screen and resetting the machine. A few common problems with the Display Screen include the LCD being unresponsive, the screen stuck on the End User License Agreement, the display screen being pixelated, and the screen stuck on the Tap to Zoom message. If you have any of these issues turn your machine off, then perform a hard reset. If the issue persists, contact Member Care at cricut.com where you can find phone numbers and emails to contact. It is important to take care of your Display Screen as it is a vital part of your Cricut Cutter machine.

Do I need all these tools?

While these tools are all great in helping you create a project, you will be glad to know that you do not need to have every single tool mentioned above to use a Cricut effectively. However, among the must-have items are the mat and the tools mentioned in the Essential Tool Set. These are extremely helpful to complete your projects especially the ones with tiny cuts. A good way to begin your Cricut crafting journey is to equip yourself with the basics, such as the mat, the Tweezer, and the Weeder to start off and then slowly add on other items.

Where do I get these supplies?

One of the best ways to score a good deal with Cricut supplies that are good quality and the right ones is directly from Cricut. By signing up for their emails, you will be informed of any sale or discounts that Cricut has all the time. You can also go online and look out for crafters' blogs and craft sites that use Cricut, and you'll find codes that you can use to get 10% discounts on your purchases. Not only that, you can get free shipping. You can also check out your local craft store to see if there are any items at the clearance section. Do take note though that some codes offered by crafts stores may not be applicable on the Cricut online store.

Another good place to purchase discounted or cheap Cricut supplies is on Amazon and even eBay.

Chapter 4: Setting Up the Machine

I am going to help you set up your machine and we will make it as easy as possible so that this will not only go smoothly but so that you can enjoy your machine without frustrating yourself. There are two different ways to do this and it depends on what technology you are working with. If you are working with a Mac or a Windows you need to set it up one way, and if you are running on an Android or an iOS you will have to do it another way. Many people think that this process is hard but it's actually quite simple and takes ten steps or less which is great right? How easy is that?

However, in case the door does not open automatically, put mild pressure on it to completely open the door. Then, place the keyboard overlay on the top of the keypad of the machine. At this point, the cartridge of the machine should be inserted into the cartridge slot.

The cartridge slot can be found in the front of the Cricut machine. However, you must ensure the title on the cartridge is in consonance with the one on the keypad overlay.

The first way we will show you how to how to set up your machine if your working with an Android or an iOS. We will go step by step in this section so that the process is able to go smoothly and without repeating steps. This can be a very frustrating thing when you are trying to set things up and this is something that we want to avoid. So let's get started so you can get your machine ready.

Plug your machine in and Turn the power on.

You will need to pair your device (either Android or iOS) with your machine. You are going to need to utilize your Bluetooth to do this.

Download the Design Space App. You will need to install it into your machine as well.

Hit the button that says menu.

Select the button that says machine setup and app overview. Now, you are going to select the button that says new machine setup.

The next step is pretty simple because the only thing that you will have to do is follow what your screen says. There are going to be on-screen promptings that will help you to complete the setup. Just be sure that you are following them accurately and if you can't go quickly that's fine. Go at the pace that your comfortable with so that you can make sure that you understand what it is they are wanting from you. Going slower will help eliminate mistakes but if you do make mistakes don't feel bad. This happens to people every day and it's easily fixable.

You will know that you've done everything right and correctly when it is telling you that it's time to make your first project. Once this happens, you know that your setup is complete. Once you've done this it's time to get crafting!

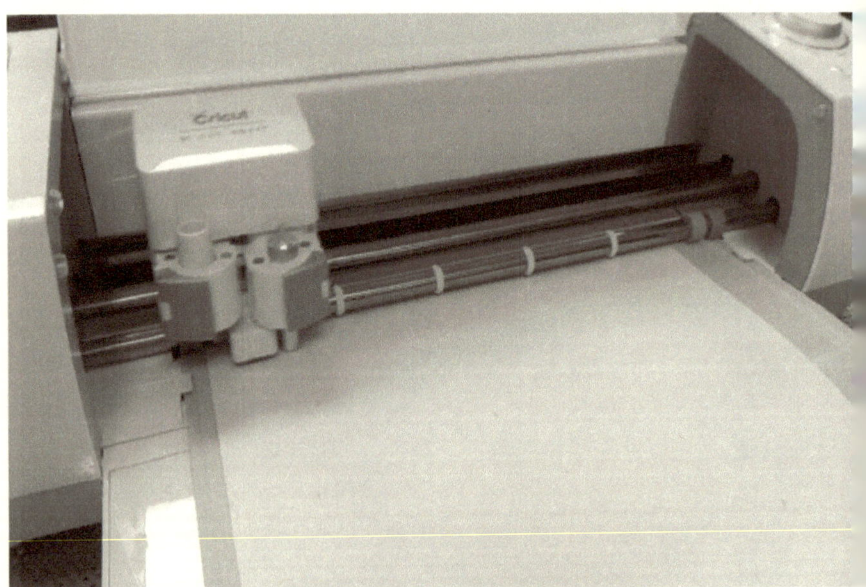

An additional tip for you is that your machine is already automatically registered during the setup. If you don't complete the setup when you connect your machine you need to reconnect it. Because the machine has to be registered this is something that you can't miss.

If you're working with a Windows or a Mac you will need to follow these following instructions to make your machine work. This setup is easy as well and offers one less step than the instructions above and since Macs are considered to be newer this will be a little bit different than the instructions above.

Plugin your machine. Don't turn your machine on or try to without plugging it in first.

Power the machine on

Connect your machine to your computer. You are going to do this in two different fashions. This is a great option because you can choose which option is the best for you. You can either do this by using the USB cord and do it this way or you can connect your machine by pairing it by using Bluetooth. Either of these ways will work well it's just whatever you would like it to be.

Go to the website design.cricut.com/setup in your browser because this is going to be how you are going to finish your set up. From this step, you will be able to complete your setup by making sure you are watching the instructions carefully.

You need to be able to follow the on-screen prompts and instructions to sign in and create your ID. This will be your Cricut ID for the future.

Download the Design Space app and install it to the device. This is going to have so much benefit for you later as this is where you are going to gain a lot of benefits.

Don't forget that you will need to plugin when it prompts you to do so.

You will be able to see that you did everything right and correctly when it wants you to make your first project. Once you reach this step your machine is ready to go, and you can make the practice project so that you can get used to your machine and how it works without wasting materials.

The same tip above about the registration applies here too and if you have a problem setting up on any of the systems you can come back to this site so that you can be able to set it up without trouble or issues. Having the website tell you what you need to do and having the prompts is a great helper to new users or older users of the machine as they offer help pages as well. With simple steps and back up help however starting your machine is easy as can be which is a great benefit to the user. These models are made to be as user-friendly as possible to eliminate the issues that other companies have when their items are being set up.

By now you should have the app installed on your phone or the software already running on your laptop or desktop computer. If you have not yet, you better do so now because things are about to get a lot more serious, and it would help if you have Cricut Design Space in front of you to experiment what we will be discussing.

What's more, you should do this, especially if you are a beginner. Perhaps intermediaries or fairly experienced users can afford not to have the app or software in front of them right now.

Downloading/Installing

Do you actually know where to get the Cricut Design Space? Well, if you are on a desktop or Personal Computer, navigate to https://design.cricut.com. If you are using an iOS device such as an iPhone or iPad, find your way to your App Store and input "Cricut Design Space" on the search space.

If your smartphone runs on Android OS, enter the Play Store and use the same search term. Remember that downloading or installing this is completely free of charge. Also, bear in mind that you will be needing a Cricut ID to sign in. This you can also get for free, even if you do not have a Cricut. Simply follow the prompts provided.

Once you have entered your email and gotten your ID, you will at once be taken into the main domain of the Cricut Design Space, the place where all of the magic happens. Quick tip: bookmark this page to your web toolbar so you can find it easily whenever you want to.

The Canvas you will be shown after - similar to a painter's whiteboard - is the big space where all your designs and progress will reflect - this space has a full grid by default to allow you see everything about a single work without having to pinch-zoom and un-pinch. Nevertheless, you can choose the appearance and measurements of the grid.

Smart guides And Shortcuts

So you want to try out your first design, and you happen to be stuck while trying to perfectly position something on your canvas? In Cricut Design Space, this could happen because the Smart Guides are just too smart for their own good. Want to know what the guides are about?

Quick one: Smart Guides are a feature of the Android and iOS app version of the product. They are designed to help you when you want to position things in relation to other things. But that could not turn out or position the way you want it to. If you want to turn this off on the app version, go to Settings - at the bottom areas of the toolbar - and toggle the Smart Guides off.

Meanwhile, there's something about the desktop version of Cricut Design Space that makes it somewhat cool - it has some keyboard shortcuts that will definitely come in handy. If you want to see them at any point of use, tap on the question mark key on your keyboard - Shift + . *Shortcuts that will prove useful to you include the show*hide menu, toggle grid, and select all options.

Other shortcuts also allow you to save and "save project as", undo - this is something you will be thankful for - redo, cut, copy, and paste. What's more, bring forward, send back, bring to front, send to back, and of course, delete.

If you are the kind of technophile who's more used to the keyboard than clicking on a mouse, you will find these shortcuts super useful.

How To Position Items On The Cricut Canvas

Not to discourage anyone, but it can take you several months of using the Cricut Design Space almost every day before you will find this useful, and probably a little more time before you can get used to it.

Well, this little nugget actually informs you on how to move and rotate your items on the mat preview. This is done in order to position your cuts and pen write when you want or feel the need to.

You know when you are working on a project and just want to flip things up fast? This feature lets you do so quickly and effortlessly - well, almost (insert smirk emoticon here).

This comes significantly handy when you want to use up scraps and just spread them all over your canvas. If you are working on an address envelope, for instance, you can use this tool so that your letters reflect on the "write" side on the envelope. You may also want to reposition - do so by tapping and dragging an item on your canvas to a new location. Simple enough, isn't it?

On the desktop version, move the objects to another mat and conceal them altogether - just click on the three dots, they are not hard to find since they are virtually in your face. So, now you know how to best position those items to make your design all the more easier. Now, on to the next on our list.

Do You Want To Sync Your Colors?

Even newbie designer knows the essence and impact of colors. In Cricut Design Space, you need to make sure your colors are happy and in harmony, just like every other artwork.

If you have ever worked on a design that had up to five different shades of pink that all needed to be cut out on separate pieces of paper or vinyl, you would understand what we are talking about. If not, you will understand soon too.

Well, in case you do not know or probably forgot how it feels, it can be very frustrating. It becomes ironic when you develop a red face that terribly matches with the moment.

Thanks to the syncing color feature, you can get all these shades and tint to match one another. Use the Color Sync option in the desktop version by simply clicking on "Color Sync" which appears at the top of the panel on the right side.

When you do this, Cricut Design Space will show you all the colors being used in your project, and then you will be able to manage them in the best possible way.

For Android and iOS users, tap on the Sync icon in the lower toolbar to have access to the same set of options. Color-syncing makes you work look more unified and professional, by the way.

Showing Others What You Are Working On

You would want others to have a sneak peek at your design in Cricut. If you have followed design freaks and enthusiasts, you would want to show them what you have been able to whip up, probably to tell you what you should add and remove.

Well, sharing is very possible, as long as the canvas on which you are currently working does not contain any uploaded files such as SVG files. Also make sure that you have not disabled the "Public" option.

If all these things are in place, then absolutely nothing is stopping you from sharing your design, except, of course, you change your mind.

First, make sure you have saved the project. Navigate the Cricut Design space to your Saved Projects location. Find the project you want and click on the Share option.

This will automatically provide you with a link you can send to people you want to see the project. It is just like the conventional infogram share option everyone is using nowadays. You can share your design with others only on the desktop and iOS version.

We are still waiting for the developers to include the same option in the Android app version of the design. But before that, sharing is easy as peasy, and I am sure Android's child will be too.

How To Remove Parts Of A Current Design

Many Cricut Design Space users have taken to social media to ask how they can remove some bits of their design when they do not want it. Actually, when you do not know what to do and how, this can be a hard nut to crack. But not for any longer.

You can remove some fragments of your progressing or finished design whenever you want, because the space has a feature that lets you do so. This feature is called Contour - you may have come across this somewhere and did not have the slightest idea that this is what it is used for. Or maybe you have not come across it at all.

To use it, just open your design in Cricut Design Space and click on the Contour button - you will see this description in the lower part of the right corner on your desktop. If you are using the mobile application version, tap on Actions, and you will see the Hide Contour option.

What next? Simply tap or click (on both app and desktop, respectively perhaps) on the bits you want to remove, and Cricut Design Space will do the rest by hiding them. Remember to save the changes once you are done "editing." This feature often works best on the desktop and iOS app versions. So if you are using the Android-based model, this should give you a heads up.

Uploading Personal Images And Rearranging Layers

Well, JPG, PNG, GIF, and BMP images can be used in the Cricut Design Space. What's more, you can easily remove the background if you want to.

This comes in very handy when you want to get nearly any kind of shape for the cutting you desire. What do you do? If you do not have the image already, look up for some of your choicest online.

When you find the one that works for you, go ahead to upload it on your canvas. There are clean up tools available for you to clean up the background to prevent interference with your project. This feature has no version bounds, as it works both on desktop and app versions (both iOS and Android).

When it comes to rearranging your layers, Cricut Design Space also has you covered. Case in point, you could just be working on a wedding invitation card projects, and you will find that the parts are overlapping.

This can cover up bits of the design you need to see to make sure you are getting it right. Well, this is something that can be fixed. Select the exact object and click Arrange, after which you should choose the Move Backward or Move Back option.

If you are using the desktop version, tap on Edit > arranged > Move Backward. Whatever be the mischief, it will surely be managed. You can now go on with your work without the layers poking out into your eyes.

If you invest in a Cricut and do not know how to master the Design Space, the investment will be futile. You will always need this software before you can think of actually cutting anything.

By now you may be wondering where the whole Cricut Access thing just came out from all of no sudden. Well, it is important that you get familiar with it at this stage so we do not get stuck explaining things that we could have in a simpler way. Actually, there is some sort of confusion regarding these two - there is the Cricut Design Space, and there's Cricut Access. Most people confuse one for the other, almost all of the time.

The difference between them, however, is that Cricut Design Space is the free software (emphasis on free) that allows you upload your projects, give them some touches and finally transfer the finished work to your Cricut machine for them to be cut.

Now, Cricut Access is the one which you have to pay for. It gives you membership and access to a butt load of graphics, fronts, and ready-to-cut projects that can be used within the Cricut Design Space.

Even if you do not have Cricut Access membership, you will still be able to see and make use of all the graphics offered by the Cricut Design Space. Be as it may, you will need to put in a few bucks for those digital files when you send your project out for the cutting. When you are charged for something, it is always clear whether the money is worth it or not.

Depending on your discretion, you may not want to have to pay for or have the Cricut Access. If that's the case, stay clear from these designs. With just the Design Space, which comes at no cost, remember, you can upload your designs and use your own fonts. You can as well create minimal designs playing with the commonest shapes such as circles, squares, and triangles.

When you purchased your Cricut, you may have been offered a 30-day free trial for Cricut Access.

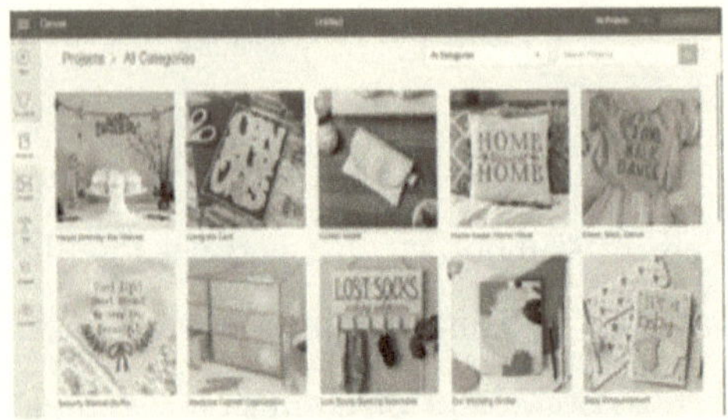

Cricut Access is a subscription-based program that gives you access to images and fonts without an extra charge, provided your subscription is up-to-date. The images and fonts are only available to those with an active subscription and if you don't pay, you'll no longer have access. The subscription is use-only; it does not allow you to keep the images and fonts. That is a common misconception.

How much you use your machine will determine if it's worth it for you to subscribe. If you're a heavy user and make a lot of different items, then a monthly or annual subscription might be right for you. This is a good choice if you're a crafter making a variety of items to sell.

If you've decided a subscription is the way to go, there are three options:

The monthly basic plan currently costs $9.99 per month and is billed monthly. The annual plan is $7.99 per month with a one-time annual billing of $95.88. The premium plan costs $119.88 annually.

Of course, you might be able to find a coupon code online and save a few dollars, and the premium subscription will give you 50% off on images and fonts not included in the basic subscription.

Cricut Design Space is the online stage that Cricut designed to be utilized with their more up to date machines.

It's not programming – you download a module on your PC (or the application on your table/telephone), and after that, you can design however much you might want.

You can utilize designs and pictures that are now transferred into Design Space, or you can transfer your own!

Cricut Design Space is 100% free. You do need to make a record; however, if you would prefer not to, you don't need to spend a penny.

Cricut Design Space is an online programming program that enables you to interface with your cutting machines through USB or Bluetooth. It's the way you make the majority of the wonderful designs that will wind up on your tasks, shirts, cushions, espresso cups, and the sky is the limit from there!

Is Cricut Access Value For The Dollar?

If you need some push to use your cutting machine more often, then maybe the Cricut Access is worth the money. It is also good if you do not know how to illustrate or create your own projects, as well as when you would rather not search for free projects on the internet.

Some people just love to design and create their own projects rather than paying someone else to do it for them. For some users, designing is only half of the fun. If you are in the habit of or want to create your own illustrations and projects, then you do not need the Cricut Access.

You also do not need it if you are willing enough to scout the internet for free projects and ideas. As is evident by now, even for a beginner, you do not necessarily need Cricut Access to cut something.

By and large, there are always other options you can give consideration to. Nonetheless, there is something that always needs trading off, and that is time. It can take a while before you can design and search for the ideal project to use. Depending on your level of web search skills, it can take you up to three hours to come up with something simple.

In the event where you just want to cut something immediately, it will be much easier to find a project that is ready to cut. Even if you find the most ideal project online, there's always something you will need to touch up.

And, there are extra steps for you to make sure you don't just cut, but cut the right way. Now, for that "no extra doubt" entry, you just have to have a go at the MAKE IT options and follow the instructions in order to cut.

If you really think having Cricut Access will surely make your design life a lot simpler and that you can enjoy the fun associated with cutting and putting together your project, then there should be nothing stopping you - the membership should very well be worth every single penny.

The membership, in context, can add up. Plus it is an extra cost atop your bills, but if you look at it, you will agree that you spend some $10 on things you do not need, probably so many silly stuff.

You spend money on things like that, so to justify every dollar, you can cut down on them and invest in Cricut Access.

Lastly, if you are as well planning to buy more materials, accessories, and machines from Cricut, know that they have great discounts for Cricut Access Members.

Chapter 5: Choosing first project ideas

Starting a New Project

When starting a new project, you'll want to know what that project will be and what materials you will be using before doing anything else.

For example, if you want to cut vinyl letters to place on wood, you'll need to know all of your dimensions so your letters fit evenly and centered on the wood. You'll need wood that vinyl can adhere to without the risk of peeling. And you'll want to make certain that your wood is sanded and finished to your desire because you don't want any imperfections. You may find even with store-bought wood pieces advertised as ready-to-use, there are tiny imperfections.

You want to make sure when working with fabric that you know what inks or vinyls will adhere to the surface. You don't want any peeling or cracking to happen to your beautiful design.

When working with any kind of fabric, including canvas bags, you'll want to prewash for sizing because shrinkage after your design has been set can cause the design to become distorted.

If you aren't sure exactly what you want to do, have something in mind so that you aren't wasting a lot of materials by trial and error. The cost of crafting materials can add up, so you'll want to eliminate as much potential waste as possible.

If you're new to Cricut Design Space, start with something simple. You don't want to get in over your head. That's the worst thing you can do when you learn any new craft. There are many used Cricut machines for sale, and while some users sell because they upgraded, others are users who gave up. You made the investment and you'll want to get a return on that investment.

The first thing that you'll get when you launch the Cricut Design Space for the first time, is a very quick tutorial on how to insert a shape, and how to fill that shape with a colored pattern. Go ahead and run through that process a few times until you're familiar with where the various assets and options are, so you can introduce a shape into the design Space, change the Linetype, and change what the shape is filled with.

As the first step, we're going to select the "Text" option. In the text box that appears, we're going to type the phrase, "Good Vibes" and pick a font in the Design Space that you like. Do remember that some of the fonts in that list will have a cost. If you're looking for free fonts exclusively, you can choose the "System Fonts," which are the fonts that are already installed on your computer.

Using the measurements at the top of the Design Space, cut a piece of vinyl that is adequately-sized to accommodate your design. Get your light blue or light-grip Cricut Maker mat and line up your vinyl so your design will print on it. Make adjustments to where your design is in the Design Space if you need to!

Once you have your vinyl where you need it, use the rounded back of your scraper/burnishing tool to smooth the vinyl down on the gripped surface, working from the middle out toward the edges. Ensure that the piece is lying flat with no bubbles or wrinkles so you get the crispest and precise cuts possible.

Once the Cricut C button is blinking, press it once and watch it work its magic! Once the machine has completed its cut, remove the mat from the machine and bring it to your crafting space. Using the rounded back of your scraper/burnishing tool, smooth the entire surface of the vinyl on your mat. This will help the carrier sheet hold onto the parts of your design that you don't want to weed.

Once you've thoroughly rubbed the entire piece, use your weeding tool to pick up the blanks around your letters. The background, the circles in your O and G, all the things you don't want to stick to your laptop. Once only the letters remain on the carrier sheet, cut an appropriately-sized piece of transfer tape. Using the back of your scraper, smooth the transfer tape down onto the entirety of your design. Once you've got a good grip on your design, peel the tape back from the carrier sheet.

Using some rubbing alcohol, clean the space on your laptop where you intend to place your design. Once it's completely clean, lay the design where you want it and rub it into place using the back of your scraper. Carefully peel back your transfer sheet to reveal your new design and admire your handiwork! You've just completed your first Cricut project! Look at you go!

Innovation is the catchphrase for being effective in the microstock business. To stand apart from the group and be seen, it is basic to separate yourself from the rest. The best way to do so is to consider new ideas and understand things from with a better point of view. I need to impart to you three different ways by which you can fire your reasoning aptitudes and concoct progressively unique thoughts and motivations.

Ways To Make Your First Art Sale Online

Put Your Work Out There

You can't simply post 1 or 2 pictures and hope to call that a portfolio. Accumulate your best outlines, works in advancement, and fine arts and transfer them to Instagram, Facebook, or a craftsman site. Individuals like to see collections of work.

In the long run, individuals will be keen on your work and can hardly wait for you to post your most recent sketch or painting.

Social Media

On the off chance that you keep on posting your craft, in the long run there will be a client who reverberates with that piece and at last will trade their cash for it.

Broaden Your Horizons

Perhaps website composition isn't for you, however this is only one model. You can likewise make your craftsmanship accessible in prints, shirts, scratch pad... and so on. You can go to the visual communication course and make work of art for gatherings or organizations. Perhaps the most ideal approaches to expand your perspectives is to transform your insight into instructing. Showing gives you believability in your field, yet expands your pay in light of the fact that in addition to the fact that you make cash from your classes or books, yet this gives your craft presentation and will build deals in that also.

Be Consistent

Try not to post an image of your craft, vanish for two months, and anticipate that clients should begin beating down your entryway. On the off chance that you need to make deals, you must be reliable. There's just a constrained measure of time you have on a newsfeed before your substance is lost in the general commotion and supplanted by more current stuff. So regardless of whether it feels dull in your psyche, post something very similar a few times over a couple of days.

Try not to stress over being pushy or over the top. Simply do a well disposed update every once in a while, and this puts what you need to state in the back of individuals' brains.

Chapter 6: Maintenance of the Cricut Machine

The Cricut Cutter machine needs to be kept intact in a variety of ways: the blade must be replaced, the cutting mats must be taken care of, and the machine, in general, must be kept clean.

Cutting Blade

Every single blade you use might get up to fifteen thousand individual cuts before it needs to be replaced. To prolong this number of individual cuts, place the aluminum foil onto the cutting mat and cut out a few designs. This process keeps the blade extra sharp and lengthens the life of the blade. This number of cuts can be greatly based on what types of materials that have been cut by the blade. If you are doing many projects in which thick materials need to be cut the blade will deteriorate quickly; the blade can also deteriorate quickly if you are cutting many materials on high pressure. A good way to know if your blade needs to be replaced is if the quality of your cuts starts to greatly decrease. If this happens it's best to replace the cutting blade. When replacing the blade, it is always best to get blades that are Cricut brand. Generic blades are often not the best quality and will cause you to constantly replace your cutting blade. To install the new blade once you've ordered the correct one, you need to first unplug your Cricut Cutter machine. Always unplug the machine before installing anything in your Cricut cutter. Next, you must remove the old, dull cutting blade from your Cricut Cutter machine. The process of how to do this has been mentioned numerous times in this book and in the last chapter. Once the cutting blade assembly has been separated it is now time to eject the blade. Find the small silver button above the adjustment knob and press the button down; this will eject the cutting blade. Be very, very careful when doing this as the blade is extremely sharp and can easily cut through the skin. Keep all blades away from children and pets. To put in the new blade, insert the blade on the end of the blade assembly opposite of the blade release button. The blade will then be pulled up into the assembly. Place the assembly back into the machine by reversing the process previously written about in the last chapter.

Subscribe to Cricut Access

If you really want to get a full range of use out of both your Cricut Explore machine as well as the Cricut Maker machine, we would recommend you subscribe to Cricut Access right away. There are two options for payment. You can either pay a monthly fee of $10, or you can pay one time for the entire year. This works out to be slightly cheaper on a month to month basis. This will give you access to thousands of different predesigned projects as well as Cricut Access exclusive fonts, that you would otherwise have to pay to use. If you are planning to use your Cricut a lot, this will save you a lot of money as opposed to buying every project an image individually. We can all agree it is a lot easier to pay one flat rate instead of having to figure out how much you are actually spending on projects. Get your money's worth out of your Cricut and subscribe to Cricut Access.

The Circuit Explore machine will come with a green 12"x12" Standard grip cutting mat. The Cricut Maker machine will come with a blue light grip mat. As you already know, you will place your cutting material onto this mat before inserting it into the machine to cut. As you will come to find out, the green cutting mat is extremely sticky when it is brand new.

Keep Your Cutting Mat Covers

The cutting mats that you purchase for your projects will always come brand new with a plastic protecting sheet over it. This can be pulled off and put back on for the entire life of the mat. You will want to keep this plastic cover as long as you have the mat. It will keep the stickiness level up on your mat, and it will make the mat easier to store away when not in use.

Cutting Mat

The Cutting mat in addition to the cutting blade needs to be taken care of. One cutting mat can have a life of anywhere from twenty-five to forty cuts. The life of the cutting mat can vary from this amount depending on the pressure and speed at which the cuts have been made and it the type of materials that have been cut on the mat. To prolong the life of your cutting mat, remove any debris from the mat after a cut and always avoid scraping the mat. If you scrape the mat, it can push any debris further into the mat. After each craft, it is best to run lukewarm water over the mat and dab it dry with a towel afterward. When a material can do not adhere to the cutting mat any longer then it is time to finally replace the mat. It is recommended to get many cutting mats and rotate between them to prolong the life of all the cutting mats. This extends the life of the mats because one cutting mat will not be cut on for many, many projects in a small amount of time. It is also recommended that you keep all of your cutting mats and all of your cartridges and blades in a very organized manner. Throwing the components of haphazardly can destroy and deteriorate them so it is best to keep them in a very organized fashion. A benefit of keeping your Cricut Cutter components organized is you won't lose or damage the very expensive items that are necessary for several projects.

How to Clean a Cricut Mat

Sometimes it also depends on the materials you use that make your machine dirty. For example, using felt means you'd need to grab stray pieces using tweezers. Another great way to clean your Cricut machine is to use a lint roller across the entire machine to pick up debris, scrap vinyl, and pieces of felt. You can also use this roller on your mats.

To clean your mats, if there are any leftover residue on your mats, the general rule is to use bleach and alcohol-free baby wipes to gently wipe the mat clean and remove it from grime, glue, and dust. You can also get yourself GOO GONE. Spray this on your mat and let it sit for 15 minutes, then use a scraper tool to remove the adhesive. But do this only if your mat is very dirty. Otherwise, wet wipes will do.

Another tip to keep your mats clean is by putting a protective cover back over them when you are not using them.

Cleaning the Cricut Machine

The final thing to keep clean is the actual Cricut Cutter machine. The machine needs to be wiped down with a damp cloth. Only wipe down the external panels of the machine and with the machine unplugged. Always wipe down the machine with a dry cloth after cleaning the outside of the machine. Never clean the Cricut Cutter machine with abrasive cleaners such as acetone, benzene, and all other alcohol-based cleaners. Abrasive cleaning tools should never be used on the Cricut Cutter machine either. In addition, never submerge any component of the machine or the Cricut Cutter machine into the water as it can damage the machine. Always keep the Cricut Cutter machine away from all foods, liquids, pets, and children. Keep the Cricut Cutter machine in a very dry and dust free environment. Finally, do not put the Cricut Cutter machine in excessive heat, excessive cold, sunlight, or any area where the plastic or any other components on the Cricut Cutter machine can melt.

Cleaning and Care

Cleaning your machine is very important, and you should do it regularly to keep everything in tip-top shape. If you don't take care of your machine, that's just money down the drain.

But what can you do to care for your machine? Well, I do suggest initially that you make sure to run maintenance on it as much as you can and keep it clean. There are a few other tips and tricks that can help prolong the machine's life. For starters, keep liquids and food away from the machine – never drink or eat while you use your Cricut machine. Set up your machine in a location that's free of dust and try to keep it away from excessive coolness or heat, so don't just throw it in the attic or an especially cold basement. If you're transporting your machine to use it at a different location, never leave it in the car. Excessive heat will melt the machine's plastic components, so be careful.

Finally, make sure the machine is stored away from sunlight. Keep it out of places in the home where sunlight hits it directly. For example, if you have an office that is very bright and the sun warms the machine for a long period of time, you'll want to move it so that it doesn't get damaged.

Be gentle with your machine. Remember, it is a machine, so you'll want to make sure that you do take some time and try to keep it nice and in order. Don't be rough with it, and when working with the machine parts, don't be too rough with them, either.

Caring for your machine isn't just about making sure that the parts don't get dirty, but you should also make sure that you keep everything in good working order.

Ensure your machine is on stable footing.

This may seem pretty basic, but ensuring that your machine is on a level surface will allow it to make more precise cuts every single time. Rocking of the machine or wobbling could cause unstable results in your projects.

Ensure no debris has gotten stuck under the feet of your machine that could cause instability before proceeding to the next troubleshooting step!

Redo all Cable Connections

So your connections are in the best possible working order, undo all your cable connection, blow into the ports or use canned air, and then securely plug everything back into the right ports. This will help to make sure all the connections are talking to each other where they should be!

Completely Dust and Clean Your Machine

Your little Cricut works hard for you! Return the favor by making sure you're not allowing gunk, dust, grime, or debris to build up in the surfaces and crevices. Adhesive can build up on the machine around the mat input and on the rollers, so be sure to focus on those areas!

Check Your Blade Housing

Sometimes debris and leavings from your materials can build up inside the housings for your blades! Open them up and clear any built-up materials that could be impeding swiveling or motion.

Sharpen Your Blades

A very popular Cricut trick in use is to stick a clean, fresh piece of foil to your cricut mat, and run it through with the blade you wish to sharpen. Running the blades through the thin metal helps to revitalize their edges and give them a little extra staying power until it's time to buy replacements.

Cleaning the Machine Itself

In general, the exterior is pretty easy to clean – you just need a damp cloth. Use a soft cloth to wipe it off, and keep in mind that chemical cleaners with benzene, acetone, or carbon tetrachloride should never be used on your Cricut machine. Any cleaner that is scratchy, as well, should be avoided at all costs.

Make sure that you never put any machine components in water. This should be obvious, but often, people may use a piece of a damp cloth, thinking that it'll be fine when in reality, it isn't.

You should consider getting some non-alcoholic wipes for cleaning your machine. Always disconnect the power before cleaning, as you would with any machine. The Cricut machine can then be lightly wiped down. Some people also use a glass cleaner sprayed on a cloth but do be careful to make sure no residue builds up. If you notice there is some dust there, you can typically get away with a cloth that's soft and clean.

Sometimes, grease can build up – you may notice this on the cartridge bar if you use cartridges a lot. Use a swab of cotton or a soft cloth to remove it.

Greasing the Machine

If you need to grease your machine, first make sure that it's turned off and the smart carriage is moved to the left. Use a tissue to wipe this down, and then move it to the right, repeating the process again.

From there, move the carriage to the center and open up a lubrication package. Put a small amount onto a Q-tip. Apply a thin coating, greasing everything evenly, and also clean any buildup that may have occurred. This is usually the issue if you hear grinding noise when cleaning the machine itself.

Never use spray cleaner directly on the machine, for obvious reasons. The bar holding the housing shouldn't be wiped down, but if you do notice an excessive grease, please take the time to make sure that it's cleaned up. Remember to never touch the gear chain near the back of this unit, either, and never clean with the machine on, for your own safety.

Cricut machines are great, but you need to take care in making sure that you keep everything in rightful order.

Cutting Blade

Your blades will tend to dull over time, but this is usually a very slow process. The best way to prevent it is to have different blades to cut different materials. Having a different blade for each material is a really good idea.

You can get fine-point ones which are good for smaller items; deep-cut, which is great for leather and other fabrics; bonded fabric, so great for fabric pieces; a rotary blade for those heavy fabrics; and finally, a knife blade, which is good for those really thick items.

In order to maintain your blades, you should clean the housing area for every blade after each use, since they get gunky fast. Squirting compressed air into the area is a wonderful way to get the dust out of there.

Cutting Mat

Your cutting mats need to be cleaned because if you don't clean them frequently, they will attract dirt and lose adhesiveness. That means you'll have to spend more money on mats, which isn't ideal. There are different ways to clean them, and we'll go over a few of the different means to clean your mats so you can use them for longer.

Cleaning the Mat Itself

First, if your mat is completely filthy, you need to clean it. Of course, you'll also want to do this for just general maintenance, too. Once it's been cleaned, you'll notice it's sticky again.

Typically, washing it down with either a magic eraser or a kitchen scrubber can do it. Sometimes, if it's really dirty, you might want to get some rubbing alcohol onto a wipe. If you notice a chunk of the debris left behind, however, is fabric oriented, then get some lint rollers or even just stick some scotch tape on there and pull it off. This can eliminate the issue.

Chapter 7: How to Cut vinyl in cricut machine

Vinyl has turned out to be well known because of its usability, assortment of hues and measure of sizes and lengths. The same number of us are very cost cognizant, we need the best esteem when obtaining our Cricut supplies. Reward projects help lessen the general expense of our provisions while exhibiting our dedication to client inviting organizations that attempt to perceive our buys.

Vinyl Cricut prizes are much increasingly explicit and accommodating. Since vinyl has such a significant number of employments in the art advertise, Cricut vinyl merchants are compensating their clients with dynamic limits dependent on the measure of the buys and their consistency. Some vinyl Cricut providers offer subsidiary projects that pay clients for advancing and publicizing their Cricut vinyl supply sites to their companions and partners. Everybody adores a lot and what arrangement is superior to FREE vinyl for your Cricut. Sharing takes brief period and exertion for such an incredible advantage.

Imaginative document sharing is fun and prizes the individuals who are eager to give others a chance to give a shot the very Cricut vinyl ventures they made. As you invest energy making recollections for yourself, you can likewise get significant Cricut rewards that help pay you back for your innovative time!

There are a few pass on cutting machines available, including the Cuttlebug and Sizzix. These machines utilize the customary strategy for kick the bucket cutting which includes putting paper over a format, covering it with a defensive board, and running it physically through a press machine to punch out the shape. This strategy has demonstrated powerful and can cut numerous impressions of a picture without a moment's delay. Be that as it may, there are a few impediments with regards to choice, stockpiling, and size.

The Cricut machine has redesigned the universe of pass on cutting. It is a totally electronic machine. The conventional bites the dust have been supplanted with little cartridges jam-stuffed with pictures and choices. The round is like a USB thumb drive in that it has a little plug that additions into the front of the machine, stores mass measures of information on it, is short, simple to store, and is compact. The Cricut capacities by having the client embed the cartridge, spread the machine keypad with the custom cartridge keypad and select the pictures wanted. By utilizing the round, the client has more choices. They can print products of the equivalent or various models, pick enhancements like shadows or italics, and in particular adjust size! The capacity to modify the size is perhaps the best element of the Cricut machine furnishing the client with the opportunity to change a picture to accommodate their plan format, not the a different way.

How to Make Multiple Layer Vinyl

Working with multiple layer vinyl can be difficult since aligning each layer individually can be a nightmare. Not to mention the effort that can go into each design only for the project to become a disaster because of poor alignment. However, there is a trick that can help you align each layer and ensure that your design will be on point. For this, we will take a closer look at so-called "alignment marks". This method is pretty known in the advanced designer community. Luckily for you, this is your chance to join the club.

Step 1: After you added your image you have to ungroup each color in separate layers.

Tip: If you want to check how many colors your image has, you can always check the "Color Sync" tab next to the "Layers" tab.

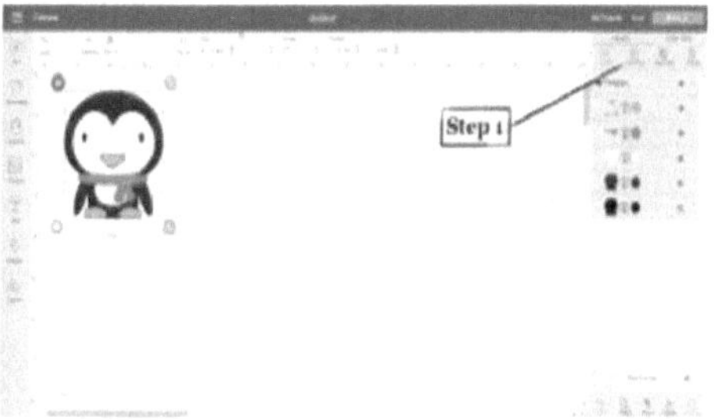

Step 2: Add a square shape with the "Shapes" tool.

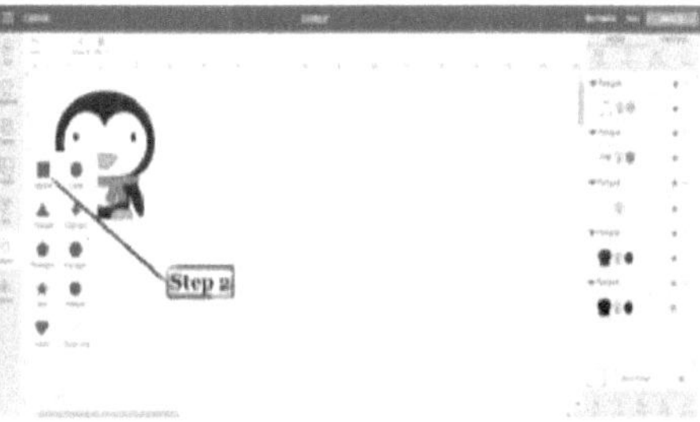

Step 3: Position it under the image and reduce its size as shown in the picture below.

Tip: Don't forget to click the "Lock Ratio" symbol on the left corner of your shape to be able to resize it properly.

Step 4: Duplicate the newly added shape.

Step 5: Select both shapes and align them horizontally.

Tip: To maneuver the objects more easily, you can weld the two rectangular shapes together.

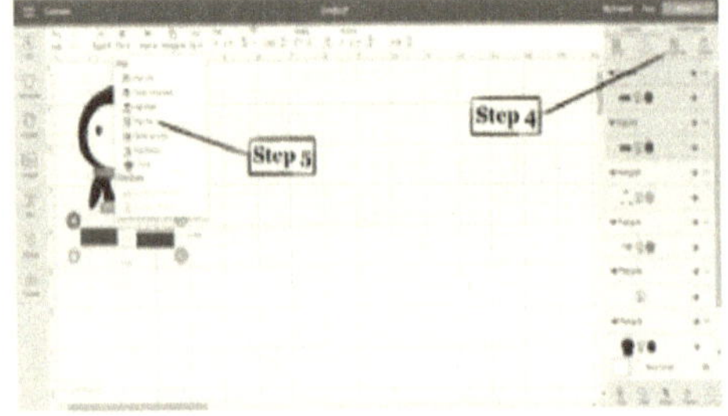

Step 6: Select all objects (image layers and welded shapes) and duplicate them. In the end, you want to have a duplicated set for each individual color. In this case, we need four sets.

Step 7: Once you duplicated the image you need to reposition them so you

can save space on the cutting map. After that delete the layers from each set so that you will be left with a different color for each vinyl group.

Once the appropriate layers are deleted you should be left with a single colored object from each set. That way you can ensure that you have all the components required for your multiple layer design.

Step 8: Select all objects and weld them together.

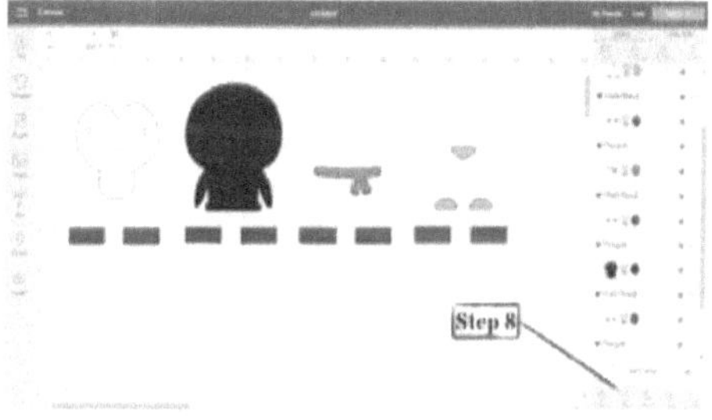

Step 9: Select "Make It" so you can get an overview of your cutting map.

Step 10: On the actual cutting map, you will want to position your colored vinyl according to the color of each object.

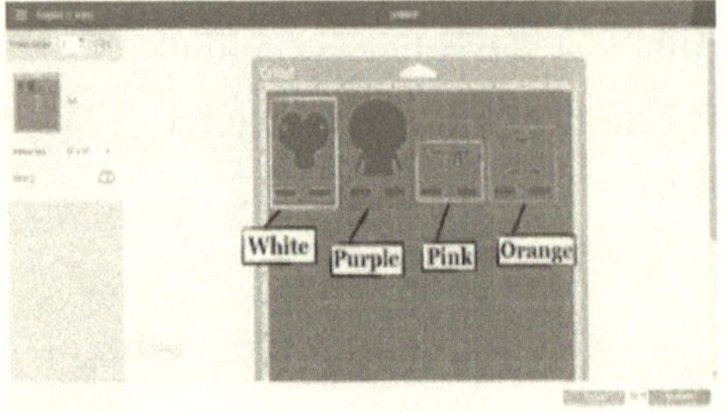

Result: Once the objects are cut out from each vinyl piece you can use the alignment markers to properly align the objects. That way you can ensure that your design will be perfectly overlapped.

Chapter 8: Making Stickers with Cricut Machine

Making Sticky Labels

Supplies needed are as follows:

- Cricut machine
- Printable sticker paper
- Inkjet printer

Take the next few steps to bring this sticker to life:

- Select the font of your desire from the available font package.
- Highlight the texts and change the color by using the available colors on the color tray.
- Click on the Print option to change the file to a print file from a cut file.
- Click on the Ungroup icon to adjust the spacing of the text.
- After adjusting the spaces, highlight all and use the Group icon to make them one whole piece again.
- Click on the Shape icon and insert a shape.
- If it's a rectangle you need, insert a square, unlock the shape, and drag it to a rectangle.
- Change the shape's color using the color tray.
- Highlight the text and use the Align drop-down box.
- Make use of the Move to Front icon to move the text to front.
- Highlight the design and click on Group.
- Duplicate the label as much as you want.
- Highlight the whole design and use the Flatten icon to keep it together during printing.
- Highlight the design and right-click then select Attach.
- Click on the Go button and print the design on the printable sticker

paper.

Steps for Making Planner Sticker

Supplies needed are as follows:

- Cricut machine
- Printable sticker paper
- Inkjet printer

Below are the steps to be taken in completing this process:

- Click on the Text icon and input your text.
- Select the font of your desire from the available font package.
- Highlight the texts and change the color by using the available colors on the color tray.
- Click on the Print option to change the file from a cut file to a print file.
- Click on the Ungroup icon to adjust the spacing of the text.
- After adjusting the spacing, highlight all and use the Group icon to make them one whole piece again.
- Click on the Shape icon and insert a shape.
- Change the shape's color using the color tray.
- Highlight the text and use the Align drop-down box.
- Make use of the Move to Front icon to move the text to front.
- Highlight the design and click on Group.
- Highlight the whole image and use the Flatten button to solidify the design as one whole piece.

How to Make Vinyl Sticker Car Window

Supplies needed are as follows:

- Cricut machine
- Premium outdoor glossy vinyl
- Transfer tape
- Scraper tool

Follow these steps to create:

- Get and save the image you want to use online.
- Select the parts of the image you do not want as part of the final cut.
- Select the image as a cute image. You will get to preview the image as a cut image.
- Approve the cut image. You would be redirected to the first upload screen.
- Click on your just finished cut file, then highlight it and insert the image.
- The image is added to your design space for size readjusting. The image is ready to cut.
- Cut the image, and remove excessive vinyl after the image is cut.
- Apply a layer of transfer tape to the top of the cut vinyl.
- Clean the car window really well with rubbing alcohol to remove all dirt.
- Carefully peel away the paperback of the vinyl.
- Apply the cut vinyl on the window. Start at one end and roll it down.
- Go over the applied vinyl with a scraper tool to remove air bubble underneath the vinyl.
- Slowly peel away the transfer tape from the window.

Making Inspirational Quote Stickers

Supplies needed are as follows:

- Cricut machine
- Printable sticker paper
- Inkjet printer

Steps to creating inspirational quotes sticker:

- Select the font of your desire from the available font package.
- Highlight the texts and change the color by using the available colors on the color tray.
- Click on the Print option to change the file to a print file from a cut file.
- Click on the Ungroup icon to adjust the spacing of the text.
- After adjusting the spaces, highlight all and use the Group icon to make them one whole piece again.
- Click on the Shape icon and insert a shape.
- If it's a rectangle you need, insert a square, unlock the shape, and drag it to a rectangle.
- Change the shape's color using the color tray.
- Highlight the text and use the Align drop-down box.
- Make use of the Move to Front icon to move the text to front.
- Highlight the design and click on Group.
- Duplicate the label as much as the screen allows.
- Highlight the whole design and use the Flatten icon to keep it together during printing.
- Highlight the design and right-click, then select Attach.
- Click on the Go button and print the design on the printable sticker paper.

Chapter 9: Personalized Ideas

There is a box at the top for searching and you can type in what you want to make. For example, if you want to make a holiday card, type in the holiday card. Remember that there are many search options so try different words to try and see new pictures. The images may be different on the screen than what you see in other places because of thy change often. This company is great about constantly evolving to give you everything you need as far as awesome ideas in their project center that they are offering you.

Some of them cost money but most are free. Keep in mind that some are for cutting and others are for printing. It's fairly easy to tell you just have to look for the price at the bottom of the picture or if there is a little printer then it means it's printable. Remember, that when you just start out start slower until you get more used to the machine and how you can work it for you.

If you think you are going to use your machine a lot then you may consider subscribing to the Cricut Access Standard because it gives you more options. Once you choose your project click the button that says insert. You'll find it at the bottom of the screen. Now that you've done this your project will be in the workspace.

Once your project is in the workspace you can make any changes to it that you want for your first project. We would recommend not making any big changes because you're not used to the app yet, but as you practice you'll learn more about making different changes and adding your own flair to your projects.

In this case for a card it might be really small so you might need to make it bigger and some of them only come with an envelope to make with it or others need you to make more things to go with it. As such these are things that you're going to have to think about. If you want to make the size bigger then, of course, you're going to make it bigger and expand it.

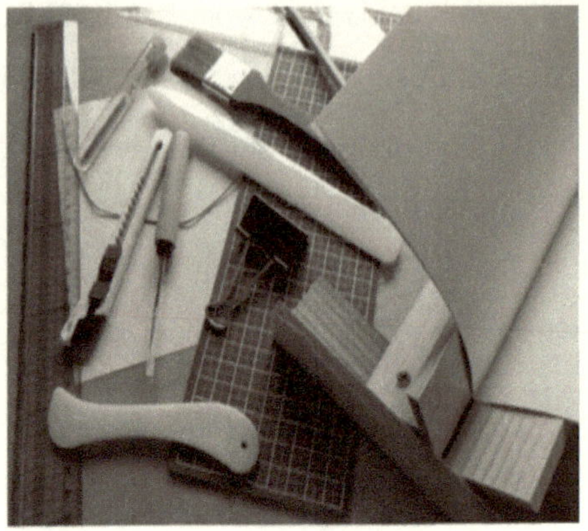

To do this you can click on the edit option at the bottom of the screen and use the width or the height section to add the changes that you want, and the app will make the changes accordingly. Once you have the size that you want and you are ready to start cutting, click the make it button.

It's going to be a green circle at the lower right part of your screen. Once you do this you'll be in the area where your product shows on the cutting mat. Click the arrow to the right and scroll through to see each mat that you can use or that you will be using. It's a good idea to look through them so that you can get your paper or vinyl-ready in the order that they will be cut. Then scroll back to the beginning and click on the continuing circle. It's going to be a green circle.

From here you can tell how the first mat is going to cut so you'll be able to get this ready. The design space will guide you through this so just follow the instructions once they pop up. Each time you start it's going to ask you to connect with a nearby device. This is a normal step so don't worry. Depending on the project you choose it could use the scoring stylus or other materials or items, so this is something to keep in mind as well. If you are using the stylus make sure that it's all the way in and it should click when it's down. Then you will need to close the latch and have it been ready. Then it's time to perform the next step.

You'll need to press the flashing buttons on the machine. This is located on the right. The first one is for loading and the second button is for cutting and for scoring. You also need to set the dial on the material that you're using.

Keep following the prompts and it will tell you when to unload and load. Then you can watch the machine cut your design. Once you've removed it from the mat you can fold it on the score lines and your project will be done. You can use the project in any way that you like but starting with something simple is really going to help you get used to spacing as well as saving materials and time.

Ready to make projects are in the app as well and all you have to do to pick one and be able to use it to your advantage is to just pick one and go with it. You pick one and then you send it to your machine and tell it to cut. Once you have this assembled you'll have a project that looks professional and glamorous in just a few minutes.

One of the things that a lot of people like to make is customized T-shirts with personalized style. So in order to do this on the machine, you would locate a ready to make a project that you like and then click on the picture. A pop-up window will open, and it'll give you all the details that you need. They give step by step instructions that you can print and keep by your side if necessary. There will be two separate buttons along the bottom that pop up.

You can customize it and make it. If you select to make it, your automatically going to be forwarded to the cut screen in your design space.

If you're working with iron-on materials, you also need to click the mirror button on each cut mat because it won't automatically see them and do it for you. If you select the customized premade design it will be loaded onto the design space canvas we talked about above. When you're here, you can edit any part of the design just as you would your own projects and this way the premade designs can be a great jumping-off point for your own unique creations. Once you're satisfied with the edits in the customization hit the green make it button to send the design to be cut. Each ready to make project includes instructions for cutting specific materials for each specific project. From there you would simply follow the instructions that pop up on the screen.

If you have the canvas screen this refers to the screen that you are going to be designing on. As such click on the new project button. Then it will open up your canvas. Now we can begin your project. There is also a zoom in and out button for you to see the details that are a little harder to see on your bottom left corner. On the left side of your screen, you will find the main buttons that are for you to use.

The new button starts a new project for you. The template button is one part that will help your project work on different items. You can change the size of the template here and the color as well.

Projects will open the different projects in the CDS. Images are where you can find the images you can buy off the app but also the images you have uploaded as well.

Shapes will show you the scoreline and shapes. You can make a plethora of different designs by adding different shapes together.

The text shows the text and helps you find the font you want on the drop-down menu.

Upload is how you upload the png, jpeg, or SVG file that you have saved on your computer.

It is a good tip to buy one thing at a time because it will keep you from getting overwhelmed in the beginning.

You also have filters, and this is a big time saver on the CDS. You can use your filters to narrow down the items that you have uploaded or the items that are available in the

Access app.

The preview screen has been recently been updated to look better and now you can move things around before you cut it on this screen as well.

You will see flatten which means that you can flatten your image together so that you are able to print it out.

Contour which means that you are deleting inside or outside of the images or unwanted lines. This is so that the images were how you want it to be.

Attach means that you are attaching text or images so that they will be cut out exactly as you have them on the canvas.

Wield is next. This wields cursive tags. So it is one continuous line and there are no tales to caught. The wheeled objects turn into one object.

The upper right-hand corner of the app has a panel too. Open it and you will the layers panel and the color sync. The color sync will let you see how many colors you have and your canvas. You can change items to the same color by dragging and dropping them in this panel. The layers panel will let you see all of the different layers of your images and you can click on the eyeball to unhide or hide certain levels.

Because most people use fonts in their Cricut machine and they want to make special T-shirts or designs, they are going to need to learn how to use the fonts and how to get them. When you are making custom designs, adding the fonts to the Cricut space is actually very easy once you know how to do it.

There are many different websites for the best fonts that you can get for free.

All you have to do to get this to work is right-click the file and then click Extract all. If you want, you can usually delete the original file to keep it from cluttering up your folders on your desktop. If you have another folder, where all of your fonts are then what you need to do is find the file on your computer and open the true type file. You will need to double click the file to open it.

This is going to open onto a view of your font. Depending on where you get your fonts from you may only receive a true type file and no other options, which are fine because your machine can still work with it. From here, you are going to need to click the install button.

You will find this at the top of the window that has just opened on your computer and then you will be able to install the font on to your computer. Now that the font is installed to your computer that is all you have to do. The next time you open up your design space you will be able to search for it and find it. When you go in the design space and you find your font after creating a text box it may or may not show up.

You can also customize your fonts in the design space as well. You can change the size of the font or the style and you can even decrease or increase the space between the letters. Another thing that you can also do is group your tags to each individual letter so that you are able to manually move each letter to exactly how you like it.

You can also find specific fonts that you need by filtering them by single layer cutting, multi-layer cutting, or by writing. This is a great find for finding fonts that have a writing option for fonts and fonts that have a writing option. You can also change how the text style looks and how the text style to writing is on the edit panel.

For fonts that have the writing option, you can also change the text to writing in the panel for editing and then you will be able to see what your text will look like when it is drawn. Make sure that you are either grouping or attaching your letters so that the text is drawn exactly the same way on the canvas otherwise your letters are going to be mixed up. So now that you have been able to understand how to add the files to your space and actually do it that is all you need to know. This is very easy and it is very basic to do once you have understood how to do it.

Machine Reset

The Cricut machine is like any other machine, and it can have problems. You may need to do a hard reset if you can't resolve the problem any other way. When troubleshooting, it's critical to follow the manufacturer's instructions. To do otherwise can damage your machine and void your warranty. For that reason, I am giving you the specific instructions from the manufacturer's website.

You want to make certain that you follow these steps in the proper order and use the instructions that are specific to your model.

Basic Object Editing

The canvas comes equipped with an editing toolbar that allows you to make corrections.

If you make a mistake, you can easily fix it. You can use the "undo" and "redo" buttons by clicking them the required number of times.

The undo icon will let you get rid of something you don't like. It acts like an eraser, and each click will undo the previous action.

If you accidentally delete something, you can use the redo button. This will restore your work.

Another editing tool is the linetype dropdown that will let you change to a cut, draw, or score object. It communicates with your machine so it knows what tools you're going to be using.

The edit icon lets you cut, copy, and paste from the canvas. It functions with a dropdown menu and you use it by selecting the elements you want to edit from your canvas.

The program also features an align tool that will let you move your design around on the canvas. If you've used a design program before, this should be easy for you to do. If you haven't, it can be tricky.

Functions of the alignment tool

The following are the functions you can use to move your design on the canvas. You might want to practice using these until you're comfortable with them.

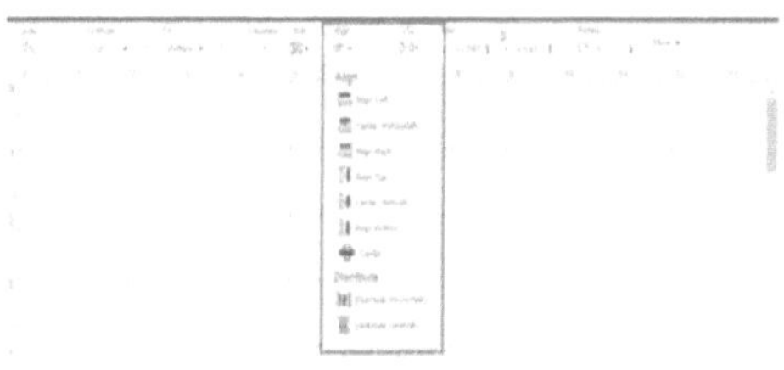

Align Left will move everything to the left.

Center Horizontal will align horizontally and will center text and images. This brings everything to the center.

Align Right will move everything to the right.

Align Top will move the designs you select to the top of the canvas.

Center Vertically will align your selections vertically.

Align Bottom will bring your selections to the bottom.

Center will bring everything to the center, vertically and horizontally.

You can also distribute vertically and horizontally. This will give you some space between your design elements.

You can also flip, arrange, rotate, and size your design. All of these features are handy, and once you master them you can quickly align your design to your preference.

Did you realize that you can change the space between letters in Cricut Design Space? This is a marvelous element that keeps clients from composing and space each letter separately. Utilize the Letter Space choice to make the space between every individual letter bigger or littler.

Changing the Space between lines of content

This choice works when there is more than one line of content in the content box, as appeared in the photograph above. Use Line Space increment or decline the space between the lines of content. This works for lines inside a similar content box.

Changing the Text Alignment

With the Text Alignment choice, clients can adjust content to one side, right, or focal point of the content box. Remember this does not adjust message inside the whole task itself, just inside the

content box.

Propelled Text Tools

The Advanced catch takes into consideration ungrouping the content. The "Ungroup to Letters" enables client to ungroup the content to individual letters. The "Ungroup to Lines" enables the client to ungroup the content to individual lines. This alternative possibly works if there is more than one line of content in the content box. If you are utilizing a multi-layer text style, then you may likewise have an "Ungroup to Layers" choice accessible. When lines or letters have been ungrouped, clients can alter and control those letters or lines autonomously.

Chapter 10: Cricut Project Ideas to Try

With Cricut, there are so many different projects that you can create. The only thing that will limit you is the amount of time and imagination you apply to each project. In this chapter, I will not only provide you with project ideas but also a few step-by-step projects to get you started. I will also provide you with images of some especially useful projects that will get those creative juices flowing.

How to Make Custom Graphic T-shirt?

First, you will need to determine what you want your shirt to say. It is best to stick with just one color when you start out. But as you get better at creating with your Cricut, you can move on to more color options in one design. Next is to pick which shirt you would like to use. This can be a preexisting shirt from your closet or it could be one that you purchased specifically for this project. The shirt needs to be a material that can be ironed.

Supplies Needed

- The Cricut machine

- Vinyl for the letters

- Your Cricut tools kit

Instructions

1.   Start by choosing the image you want to use. This can be done in Photoshop or you can place your text directly into the Design Space.

2.   Next, open the Cricut Design Space. Choose the canvas that you wish to use by clicking the Canvas icon on the dashboard which is located on the

left-hand side. Select the canvas that you will be using for your vinyl letters on. This can be anything within the categories they offer.

3.   Then, select the size of the shirt for the canvas. This is located on the right-hand side of the options.

4.   Now, click Upload for uploading your image, which is located on the left-hand side. Select the image you are using by browsing the list of images in your file library. Then, select the type of image that you have picked. For most projects, especially iron-on ones, you will select the Simple Cut option.

5.   Click on the white space that you want to be removed by cutting out. Remember to cut the insides of every letter.

6.   Next, be super diligent and press Cut Image instead of Print first. You do not want to simply print the image, you cut it as well.

7.   Place the image on your chosen canvas and adjust the sizing of the image.

8.   Place your iron-on image with the vinyl side facing down on the mat and then turn the dial to the setting for iron-on.

9.   Next, you will want to click the Mirror Image setting for the image prior to hitting go.

10.   Once you have cut the image, you should remove the excess vinyl from the edges around the lettering or image. Then use the tool for weeding out the inner pieces of the letters.

Now you will be placing the vinyl on the shirt.

1.   And now, the fun part begins. You will get to iron the image on to the shirt. Using the cotton setting, you will need to use the hottest setting that you can get your iron to. There should not be any steam.

2.	You want to warm the shirt by placing the iron on the shirt portion that will hold the image. This should be warmed up for 15 seconds.

3.	Next, lay the vinyl out exactly where you want it to be placed. Place a pressing cloth over the top of the plastic. This will prevent the plastic on the shirt from melting.

4.	Place your iron onto the pressing cloth for around 30 seconds. Flip the shirt and place the pressing cloth and iron on the back side of the vinyl.

5.	Flip your shirt back over and begin to peel off the sticky part of the vinyl that you have been overlaying on the shirt. This will separate the vinyl from the plastic backing. This should be done while the plastic and vinyl are hot. If you are having trouble removing the vinyl from the plastic backing, then place the iron back on the part that is being difficult. Then proceed to pull up and it should come off nicely.

6.	This should remove the plastic from the vinyl that is now on the shirt. Place the pressing cloth on top of the vinyl once again and heat it to ensure that the vinyl is good and stuck.

How to Make Vinyl Wall Decals?

Supplies needed are as follows:

- Adhesive vinyl
- Cricut machine
- Weeding tool
- Scrapper tool

Instructions

1. Log in to the Cricut design space.
2. Create a new project.
3. Click on Upload Image.
4. Drag the image to the design space.
5. Highlight the image and "flatten" it.
6. Click on the Make It button.

7. Place vinyl to the cutting mat.

8. Custom dial the machine to vinyl.

9. Load the cutting mat into the machine.

10.   Push the mat up against the rollers.

11.   Cut the design out of the vinyl.

12.   Weed out the excess vinyl with a weeding tool.

13.   Apply a thin layer of transfer tape on the vinyl.

14.   Peel off the backing.

15.   Apply the transfer tape on the wall.

16.   Smoothen with a scraper tool to let out the air bubble.

17.   Carefully peel off the transfer tape from the wall.

How to Make Stickers with Your Cricut?

The supplies that you will need:

- Cricut Explore Air 2

- Printable sticker paper by Cricut

Instructions

1. Log in to your Cricut Design Space account.

2. In the Cricut Design Space, you will need to click on Starting a New Project. Then, select the image that you would love to use for your stickers. You can use the search bar on the right-hand side at the top to locate the image that you want to use.

3. Next, click on the image and click Insert Image so that the image is selected.

4. Click on each one of the files that are in the image file and click the button that says Flatten at the lower right section of the screen. This will turn the individual pieces into one whole piece. This prevents the cut file from being individual pieces for the image.

5.   Now, you want to resize the image so that it is the size that you wish it to be. This can be any size within the recommended space for the size of the canvas.

6.   If you want duplicates of the image for sticker sheets, you should select all and then edit the image and click Copy. This will allow you to copy the whole row that you have selected. Once you have copied, you can then edit and paste the multiple images to make a sheet. This is the easiest way to copy and paste the image over and over again.

7.   At this time, you are ready to start printing your stickers. Click the Save button on the left-hand side of the screen to save the project and chose the option Save as Print and then Cut Image. Once done, you can click the green button that says Make It. This will be located on the section to the right of the screen.

8.   Verify that everything is how it needs to be and click Continue. This will give you a prompt to print the image onto your paper. Make sure you have used the sticker paper for the stickers. Otherwise, it won't work.

9.   Print out the image with your printer. If the Cricut sticker paper is too thick for your printer, using a thinner sticker paper is fine.

10.   After the design is printed, adjust the Smart Set dial to the appropriate setting. Place the paper onto the cutting mat and load it into the Cricut machine by pushing against the rollers. Press your Load and Unload button that is flashing.

11.   Press Go, and this will begin to cut your stickers. Since the stickers are small and intricate you will need to be patient.

12.   A tip for getting a good cut is to not touch the mat and once the first cut is made and done, repress the flashing button to re-cut the stickers on the same lines that were previously cut.

Steps for Making Planner Sticker

Supplies needed are as follows:

- Cricut machine

- Printable sticker paper

- Inkjet printer

Instructions

1. Log in to the Cricut design spaces.

2. Start a new project and click on the Images at the screen's left side. Select the image(s) you want.

3. Click on the Text icon and input your text.

4. Select the font of your desire from the available font package.

5. Highlight the texts and change the color by using the available colors on the color tray.

6. Click on the Print option to change the file from a cut file to a print file.

7. Click on the Ungroup icon to adjust the spacing of the text.

8. After adjusting the spacing, highlight all and use the Group icon to make them one whole piece again.

9. Click on the Shape icon and insert a shape.

10. Change the shape's color using the color tray.

11. Highlight the text and use the Align drop-down box.

12. Make use of the Move to Front icon to move the text to front.

13. Highlight the design and click on Group.

14. Highlight the whole image and use the Flatten button to solidify the design as one whole piece.

15. Resize the design to the appropriate size you need. You realize this by clicking on the design then dragging the right side of the box to the size you desire.

16. Click Save at the top left to save your project. Save it to be a Print and Cut image, after which you click the Make It button at the right hand of the screen.

17. Examine the end result and click Continue if it's what you expected. This will lead you to print the design onto the paper.

18.	Adjust the dial on the Cricut machine to the required settings.

19.	Place the sticker paper on the cutting mat.

20.	Load the cutting mat into the machine, and push it against the rollers.

21.	Press the Load/Unload button and then the Go button to cut the sticker.

22.	Your planning sticker is ready.

How to Make Personalized Pillows

Supplies Needed

- Black, dark blue, or dark purple fabric

- Heat transfer vinyl in gold or silver

- Cutting mat

- Polyester batting

- Weeding tool or pick

- Cricut EasyPress

Instructions

1. Decide the shape you want for your pillow, and cut two matching shapes out of the fabric.

2. Open Cricut Design Space and create a new project.

3.   Select the "Image" button in the lower left-hand corner and search "stars."

4.   Select the stars of your choice and click "Insert."

5.   Place the iron-on material on the mat.

6.   Send the design to the Cricut.

7.   Use the weeding tool or pick to remove excess material.

8.   Remove the material from the mat.

9.   Place the iron-on material on the fabric.

10.   Use the EasyPress to adhere it to the iron-on material.

11.   Sew the two fabric pieces together, leaving allowance for a seam and a small space open.

12.   Fill the pillow with polyester batting through the small open space.

13.   Sew the pillow shut.

14.   Cuddle up to your starry pillow!

How to Make Cricut Cake Toppers

Supplies Needed

- Cardstock – Glittery gold and white

- Glue stick

- Glue gun

- Lightstick cutting mat

- Weeding tool or pick

- Toothpicks

Instructions

1. Open Cricut Design Space and create a new project.

2. Select the "Image" button in the lower left-hand corner and search for

"star."

3.   Select the star you like best and click "Insert."

4.   Place your gold cardstock on the cutting mat.

5.   Send the design to your Cricut.

6.   In Design Space, select the "Text" button in the lower left-hand corner.

7.   Choose your favorite font and type, "Happy birthday!"

8.   Place your white cardstock on the cutting mat.

9.   Send the design to your Cricut.

10.   Remove the outer edge of the paper, leaving the text on the mat.

11.   Use your weeding tool or carefully pick to remove the text from the mat.

12.   Use the glue stick to attach the text on top of the stars.

13.   Use the glue gun to attach toothpicks to the back of each star.

14.   Stick your toppers onto your cupcakes!

How to Make Fabric Bookmark Made Using a Cricut

Supplies Needed

- Fabric

- Paper, and even ribbon or metal.

- Cricut

Instructions

1. Using a Design Space file that is designated for the bookmark's size, cut the fabric.

2. Start with placing the fabric on the cutting mat and running it through the Cricut with the appropriate settings.

3. If you are making more than one bookmark, then copy the bookmark

onto the Design Space within the parameters of the cutting mat.

4.   You will need 2 pieces of fabric per bookmark.

5.   Using a Cricut Maker, you are able to cut more pieces at a faster pace.

6.   Cut your interfacing fabric or cardboard into the dimensions of 6.75" h x 1.75" w with one per bookmark.

7.   Attach your fabrics together with the wrong sides facing using some pins. Sew your long sides and the bottom together. Use your foot that is for edgestitch to guide the fabric with a straight line. Sew with the needle down setting in order to pivot at the end of the corners. Make sure you backstitch the beginnings and ends of the lines.

8.   Fold the casing of your bookmark on the right side. Using a pencil, you can push the corners of the bookmark out so that it is right side out. Using your iron, press the casing to flatten.

9.   Insert the interfacing fabric that is fusible inside your bookmark.

10.   Fold over the top edge and use the iron to press it with the heat.

11.   Proceed to sew the top shut.

12.   Using the iron, press the bookmark so that it is fused and flat. The heat will fuse the bookmark and interfacing fabric.

13.   Now that you are done you will be able to make bookmarks out of fabric.

How to Make Cricut Gift bag

Supplies Needed

- White kraft paper

- Cricut Pen Tool in color(s) of your choice

- 12x24 cutting mat

- Weeding tool or pick

Instructions

1. Open Cricut Design Space and create a new project.

2. Select the "Image" button in the lower left-hand corner and search for doodled images appropriate for the gift you're wrapping, for example, "Christmas doodle" or "birthday doodle."

3. Select the images you like and click "Insert."

4. Copy, resize, and rotate the images to create a pattern you like for the size of your wrapping paper.

5.   Change the colors of the doodles if desired—leaving them black creates a coloring-book feel, or you can make them in different colors.

6.   Place your paper on the cutting mat.

7.   Send the design to your Cricut.

8.   Remove your wrapping paper from the mat.

9.   Wrap your gift in your customized wrapping paper!

How to Make Vinyl Clock?

Supplies Needed

- Vinyl record

- Old Clock machine

- Glue/gum

Instructions

1. It can be implicated in so much ways. First of all cut the vinyl record in a shape of your choice, square, triangle, flower, circle and in any shape.

2. Set the clock machine in a center of vinyl record.

3. Use glue to fix it right in the center.

4. Vinyl clock is just ready for use. Place it on your desk with by attaching some stand to it or hang it on your wall.

How to Make Leather Cuff Bracelet?

Supplies Needed

- A small piece of leather

- A bracelet or piece of chain or cord, and small jump rings

- Needle-nose pliers for jewelry

- Deep cut blade for the Cricut Explore

Instructions

1. Your first step is to choose the design image that you would like to use on your leather bracelet. This can be found inside the image files under Lace or any other design file that you already have.

2. Next, verify that the sizing is appropriate for a bracelet by cutting it on paper. You definitely do not want to cut the leather and be wrong. This would waste the materials.

3. Once the size is perfect, you are able to begin your project.

4. Place the leather on the mat with the smooth side down and push the

Cut button.

5.   After the leather piece is cut, you will need to adjust your chain or rope to the appropriate size that is needed for the wrist of the person that it will be fitting.

6.   Connect the leather to the chain with the jump rings. Attaching the links to the leather is perfectly fine, but it may tear the leather so using the jump rings is a great alternative.

How to Decorate a Mug

Supplies needed:

- Adhesive vinyl
- Cricut machine
- Weeding tool
- Scrapper tool

Instructions

1. Log in to the Cricut design space.
2. Create a new project.
3. Click on upload image.
4. Drag the image to the design space.
5. Highlight the image and "flatten" it.
6. Use the Make It button.
7. Place vinyl to the cutting mat.
8. Push up against the roller.

9. Custom dial the machine to vinyl.

10.   Load the cutting mat into the machine.

11.   Push the mat up against the rollers.

12.   Cut the design out of the vinyl.

13.   Weed out the excess vinyl.

14.   Apply a thin layer of transfer tape on the vinyl.

15.   Peel off the backing.

16.   Apply the cut design on the mug.

17.   Smoothen with a scraper tool to let out all air bubble.

18.   Carefully peel away the transfer tape.

How to Create the Stencil for Painting?

Supplies needed are as follows:

- Cricut machine
- Stencil vinyl
- Weeding tool

Instructions

1. Log in to the Cricut design space.
2. Click on the Text icon and input your text.
3. Highlight the font and change the font.
4. Ungroup the text.
5. Adjust the spacing, and let them overlap slightly.
6. Highlight and group the text.
7. Adjust the text size to the size of the stencil you want to make.
8. Highlight the text and "attach" to keep them together.

9. Click on the Insert Shape icon.

10.   Insert a square shape.

11.   Unlock the shape and make it a rectangle.

12.   Move the new shape over the text.

13.   Right-click on the box and select Move to the Back.

14.   Change the color of the shape to whatever color you want.

15.   Highlight the whole project and "attach."

16.   After attaching it all, the cut line should be shown.

17.   Press the Make It button on your machine.

18.   Place the stencil vinyl onto the cutting mat.

19.   Load the cutting mat into the machine.

20.   Let the machine cut out the design on the stencil.

21.   Weed out the excess vinyl with the weeding tool.

The stencil is ready.

How to Make Wooden Hand-Lettered Sign

Supplies Needed

- Acrylic paint for whatever colors you would like

- Vinyl

- Cricut Explore Air 2

- Walnut hollow basswood planks

- Transfer Tape

- Scraper

- An SVG file or font that you wish to use

- Pencil

- Eraser

Instructions

1. You will need to start by deciding what you will want to draw onto the wood.

2. Then, place some lines on the plank to designate the horizontal and

vertical axis for the grid. Set this aside for later.

3.   Upload the file that you wish to use to the Design Space. Then, cut the file with the proper setting for vinyl.

4.   Weed out the writing or design spaces that are not meant to go on the wood.

5.   Using the transfer tape, apply the tape to the top of the vinyl and smooth it out. Using the scraper and the corner of the transfer paper, slowly peel the backing off a bit at a time. Do it carefully.

6.   Remove the backing of the vinyl pieces, aligning the lettering or design so that it is fully centered. Place it carefully on the wooden plank.

7.   Again, use the scraper to smooth out the vinyl on the plank.

8.   Take off the transfer tape by smoothing off the bubbles as you scrape along the wood sign. Discard the transfer tape at that time.

9.   Continue to use the scraper to make the vinyl smoother. There should be no bumps since this creates bleeding.

10.   Now, paint your wood plank with any color of your choice. Peel the vinyl letters off. Once the paint has completely dried, you are able to erase your pencil marks.

How to Make Personalized Water Bottle

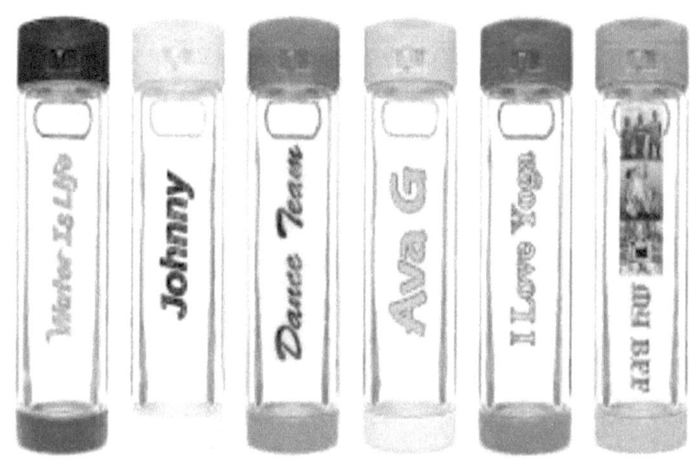

Supplies Needed

- Glue

- Vinyl lettering

- Paper

- Scissors

- Plastic bottle

Instructions

1. Preparing decorative coffee cup with the use of vinyl decorative items is no more difficult. Wrap a piece of vinyl lettering and wrap it around the coffee cup.

2. Give name of your kid on it so it may not get miss placed. Personalizing coffee cup with vinyl craft is very beautiful.

3. In same way using vinyl letters you can name drawers and cabinets of

your kitchen.

How to Make Fabric Wreath with Flowers

Supplies Needed

- A ring from an old lampshade

- Ribbon to wrap the lamp shade

- Cricut Maker

- Cricut felt in various colors

- Rotary blade

- Cricut 12x12 mat for fabric

- Hot glue gun and sticks of glue

- Felt balls

- Wreath forms

Instructions

1.   Using your Cricut Design Space you need to log in.

2.   In the Cricut Design Space, you will need to click on Starting a New Project and then select the image that you would like to use for your flowers.

You can use the search bar on the right-hand side at the top to locate the image that you are wishing to use.

3.   Next, click on the image and click Insert Image so that the image is selected.

4.   Click on each one of the files that are in the image file and click the button that says Flatten at the lower right section of the screen. This will turn the individual pieces into one whole piece. This prevents the cut file from being individual pieces for the image.

5.   Now, you want to resize the image so that it is the size that you wish it to be. This can be any size that is within the recommended space for the size of the canvas.

6.   If you want duplicates of the image for a sheet of flowers, then you should select all and then edit the image and click Copy. This will allow you to copy the whole row that you have selected. Once you have copied, you can then edit and paste the multiple images to make a sheet. This is the easiest way to copy and paste the image over and over again.

How to Make Faux Leather Tutorial

Supplies Needed

- Necklace chain

- Jewelry pliers

- Cricut gold pen

- Cricut Explore Air 2

- Cricut strong mat grip

- Cricut faux leather

- Jump ring

- Fabric fusion

Instructions

1. Start by opening the Cricut Design Space. Choose the size that you want the pendant to be. This can be a circle pendant. Using the machine, make another circular-sized pendant.

2. Attach the jump ring here later after the circles have been made.

3.   Next, open the text section in the Design shop and type in the exact initials that you would like to use.

4.   Select the section that has a writing style option from the menu and adjust the font of the lettering to whatever you wish.

5.   Drag your letter to the center part of the circle and resize it to fit the appropriate size.

6.   Be sure to make a front and a back. This will ensure both sides of the piece look like leather.

7.   Create your circle so that it matches the other one minus the letter.

8.   Make this an attached set.

9.   Using the Cricut pen, begin to cut the pieces. As it is cutting the leather, it will print the initials.

10.   Use your fabric fusion glue to join the two pieces of leather together making the pendant.

11.   Using the pliers for jewelry, you can twist on the ring for the necklace.

12.   Attach your pendant and jump ring together and then string it onto the chain.

13.   The pliers can close the jump ring off.

How to Make Feather Earrings with Faux Leather?

Supplies Needed

- Fabric fusion

- Paintbrush

- Washi tape

- Metallic paint

- Cricut Explore Air

- Cricut faux leather

- Cricut standard cutting mat

- A hole puncher

Additional supplies needed:

- Jewelry pliers

- Jump ring

- Chain

Additional earring supplies:

- Earring findings

- Jewelry pliers

Instructions

1. Use the cut file for the jewelry that you would like to cut for the pattern. Cut two pieces for each piece of jewelry.

2. Make sure that you have two pieces per item so that you can glue them together. This makes them look like leather on both sides.

3. Mirror the pieces so they match.

4. Using your washi tape, mark off a section that is the top half of the faux leather piece. Press this tape firmly in place so that you can prevent the leakage of the paint.

5. Paint the end that you would like to be painted. After it is painted, let it completely dry. Repeat for the other pieces that you are painting.

6. Once it is dried out, remove your washi tape.

7. Now, use the fabric to fuse together the two pieces of each mate. These pieces should be flawlessly fit together. Use the directions on the bottle to adhere these pieces together.

8. Using a strong needle or a micro puncher, make a hole that is small but big enough to attach the hardware.

9. Use the pliers to open the jump ring and then loop it into the earrings. Attach the jewelry to the earring pieces or the necklace pieces.

How to Make Easy Envelope Addressing

Supplies Needed

- Envelopes to address

- Cricut Pen Tool

- Lightstick cutting mat

Instructions

1.   Open Cricut Design Space and create a new project.

2.   Create a box the appropriate size for your envelopes.

3.   Select the "Text" button in the lower left-hand corner.

4.   Choose one handwriting font for a uniform look or different fonts for each line to mix it up.

5.   Type your return address in the upper left-hand corner of the design.

6.   Type the "to" address in the center of the design.

7.   Insert your Cricut pen into the auxiliary holder of your Cricut, making sure it is secure.

8.   Place your cardstock on the cutting mat.

9.   Send the design to your Cricut.

10.   Remove your envelope and repeat as needed.

11.   Send out your "hand-lettered" envelopes!

Chapter 11: Tips and Tricks

Organize your tools and label your buttons.

If you are able to you can subscribe to the access for about ten dollars a month to gain access to over twenty thousand different images and over a thousand different projects. You even get over three hundred fonts.

If you have an Air 2 the mat can be sticky. Peel off your cover and then place a dry shirt over the mat (make sure that it is clean) to prime it for your first project. What this does is it helps with that stickiness from the card stock without damaging your first project.

Set your dial as this is important. Turn it to the correct material setting. If you don't it can ruin the cuts your making because it's on the wrong one.

If you have a small design or something that's more intricate then you can use what is known as a weeding box, this is also a good idea when your cutting on one mat for multiple designs.

When you are cutting vinyl that is heat transfer you will need to remember to mirror the design.

When you are using vinyl you also need to remember that you need to place your vinyl right way up on your mat for cutting. For heat transfer place its shiny side down.

When beginning to understand the correct use of your cutting mat then you need to make sure that you are loading you mat correctly so that both sides are sliding under the rollers. If you don't do this it won't load properly.

You will also need to keep the plastic sheets that come with the mats to protect them between your uses.

Clean your cutting mats with baby wipes that are water-based to keep them sticky and clean longer.

Use one blade for your cardstock and a separate one for vinyl because this will let them both last longer.

This is going to allow you to cut through thicker materials like chipboard or leather. The blade would be compatible with the Air 2. Remember we said the Maker cuts deeper, but the others can't. This blade will help but remember to order your housing for the blade as well.

This is for people who have had the cartridges for an older machine or older cartridge. You can hook these up to your new account. It is a simple thing to do but you should know that you could only link them once so be sure that if you are buying a machine second hand that nothing has been linked yet.

This is probably going to seem like a no brainer but it's actually a serious tip that you will need to remember. Remember not to leave your pen in the machine after you've completed a project. You get so involved in what you're doing that you can forget about the supplies and the things of that nature that you leave in it there but guess what? The next time you reach for it, it will be dried out and you can't use it. Replace the cap and make sure it's not drying out. They can be expensive, and you don't want to waste them. Most projects are encouraging this tip as well because it is so important.

The right tools are important here so you should make sure that you have the toolset. It will contain vital tools that you need, and they can especially help with vinyl.

Know your glue

Many people are huge fans of what is called tacky glue. It gives your projects a little bit of wiggle room when you're trying to position them. The problem is that it can take longer to dry. If this is something that bothers you, you might want to try a quicker one. Zip dry paper glue it's extremely sticky and much faster.

A tip that will go along with the tip above is that if you want them to be a layer to pop out from another layer. You can make this happen by using products like pop dots or Zots. They are foam mounts that are self-adhesive. You can also make little circles by using craft foam or cardboard and then glue it between the layers.

You don't have to get your materials from a craft store. In all honesty, they can be quite expensive. There are ways around this (coupons, sales things like that), however, you can shop online or local sign shops. Some even offer you scraps for free in some cases. If there is something that you need such as cardstock, then you should print out the color you need and then cut it out so that you can bring it with you.

Profound Knowledge

The crude materials of configuration may be documentation, a perfect workbench, studio, easels, paints, ability, and information. A performer has to know scales. A painter needs to get tones. A stone carver needs a sharp eye for negative space. An essayist must have a feeling of style.

Figure out how to trust and pursue your impulses

In the event that you ask any effective businessman what has prompted their prosperity, they once in a while state it? They for the most part say one essential key to business achievement is trusting and following your impulses. Achievement can emerge out of basically acting naturally.

Think about a Coach

Business mentors are extremely popular nowadays. Consider going through some cash with a Scrapbooking business mentor who comprehends the business as well as genuinely comprehends the specific brand of energy scrapbook sweethearts share. A mentor can help share business abilities however can go about as an extraordinary coach in managing you to your objectives.

Exhibit Your True Talent With a Business Card for Artists

The financial downturn has left huge numbers of us feeling the squeeze. Numerous individuals are searching for approaches to set aside cash in each part of life. Be that as it may, there are times when a buy must be made, and cautious research regularly structures some portion of the basic leadership the procedure.

Give the Quality of Your Work A chance to radiate Through

A business card for specialists is your window to the world, and it should say a great deal regarding your aesthetic edge and abilities. Make it state every little thing about you and what you can offer. Plan a motivating logo that can join the substance of what you can do with an incredible structure. This astute connecting can put you on top of things by helping individuals to recollect who and what you are.

Consider Other Ways You Can Display Your Skills to the World

A business card for specialists is only one of numerous limited time apparatuses you can use to enhance your presentation. It bodes well. The production of a notice is a magnificent method to demonstrate the best of what you do. Try not to place a lot into your sign; that will go about as an obstacle and prevent individuals from getting a vibe of your actual abilities. Consider the area where you can show your blurb. Vital arranging of the setting of your sign can help augment its effect. It will expand the intrigue of your work and open up more potential outcomes.

Remember to tell individuals how to connect!

A business card for specialists needs not exclusively to demonstrate the embodiment of your innovativeness; it likewise fills a need. It needs to tell potential clients how to connect with you. Incorporate all the distinctive contact techniques you have, email, site, telephone numbers, and any online networking you are an individual from. Remember about the intensity of internet based life and bookmarking destinations; they can enable feature to considerably a greater amount of your work.

Be Adaptable

Consider chipping away at zones that you hadn't imagined, however will be something inside your abilities. This will enable you to set up a notoriety. Another viable method to advance your aptitudes notwithstanding utilizing a business card for specialists is to engage in network ventures where you offer your administrations for nothing. Make something stunning that individuals will see every day; this is an incredible advert for your aptitudes. This will place your work into the lives of thousands of individuals and will drive more clients to you.

Hard Practice

Learning alone, however, doesn't convert into aptitude. We expand on the establishment with a long stretch of time of training.

It doesn't make a difference if the training occurs at the easel, composing work area, or workbench.

Creators practice to the point that the art turns out to be natural. It resembles contact composing on the console. At the point when the dream strikes, we make without the slightest hesitation.

Learning of the User

Configuration spaces programming, similar to all structure, must focus on the client. They are the explanation behind the product in any case. Something worth being thankful for about present-day ways to deal with programming improvement, in any event in their unique pronouncements, is their acknowledgment of this reality.

They request that the client is included. They should be fused into the procedure, sharing thoughts regarding what works, what doesn't, and why.

Calm

In the wake of structure information, rehearsing hard, and figuring out how to see the world through the client's eyes, it's a great opportunity to get tranquil. Stop. Think. Sketch. Pause. Hold up some more, and in the end, the thoughts will begin streaming.

Once in a while, it takes some time. Once in a while, the musings you had during the exploration part of the improvement spring to life rapidly, however typically not. When it begins, however, it floods. Keep a note pad, a heap of paper, or an application close by. Whatever you use, hold writing down the out of this world.

Adaptability

A few people make all the more successfully on a fixed calendar. John Cheever went to a cellar office for eight hours consistently. Others of us need to make the most of current opportunities, regardless of great importance.

Tune in to your very own innovativeness, and realize what works best for you. Did you realize that you can likewise offer your imaginative plans to inside decorators or property holders who are energetic about home style? You can publicize your lucrative plans to home stores or backdrop and paint stores and leave them your business cards or flyers promoting your custom divider workmanship administration.

Conclusion

Congratulations we have come to the end of this basic design space training guide for beginners. Remember the key to mastering design space is to practice daily. We cannot possibly know it all, but we sure can aspire to have sufficient knowledge to craft out wonderful designs.

The next step is to find projects and materials that excite you and dive right in! I would love to see my readers embrace the vast number of crafting opportunities that now lie ahead of them.

Don't be scared of going into design space and playing around with everything. Allow yourself to make mistakes, learn and unlearn. Before long you would be comfortable with using it.

To be a professional in any endeavor in life requires dedicated efforts to learn and practice what you have learnt. The Cricut Design Space is, by all standard, what makes the Cricut machine to be best crafting machine in the market. With this mastery, you become a champion of champions in the crafting world.